Of Time and Place

A Farm in Wisconsin

Of Time and Place

A Farm in Wisconsin

Richard Quinney

Borderland Books

Published by Borderland Books, Madison, WI
www.borderlandbooks.net

Publisher's Cataloging-in-Publication Data
Quinney, Richard.
Of time and place: a farm in Wisconsin / Richard Quinney — 1st ed.
p. : ill. ; cm.
Includes bibliographical references.

ISBN: 978-0-9768781-2-4

1. Quinney, Richard — Family. 2. Quinney, John, 1821 — Family. 3. Quinney family. 4. Irish Americans — Wisconsin — Walworth County — Genealogy. 5. Wisconsin — Genealogy. 6. Photographs in genealogy. 7. Farm life — United States — Anecdotes. 8. Family farms — United States — Anecdotes. I. Title.
CS71.Q85 2006
929/.2/0973 2005909867

Printed in the United States of America
First edition

Home is where one starts from. As we grow older
The world becomes stranger, the pattern more complicated
Of dead and living. Not the intense moment
Isolated, with no before and after,
But a lifetime burning in every moment
And not the lifetime of one man only
But of old stones that cannot be deciphered.

T. S. Eliot, "East Coker"

So I must believe that, at least to human perception, a place is not a place until people have been born in it, have grown up in it, lived in it, known it, died in it—have both experienced and shaped it, as individuals, families, neighborhoods, and communities, over more than one generation.

Wallace Stegner, *Where the Bluebird Sings to the Lemonade Springs*

Contents

Prologue

THIS PLACE, TO WHICH I AM NATIVE, I want you to know about. I will describe this place to you in words that come as I think about and imagine the lives of those who once lived here inhabiting these few acres of rolling hills and wetlands in southeastern Wisconsin. To anyone who will listen, I have a tale to tell.

The farm has belonged to my family for four generations. Settled by my great-grandparents fleeing the potato famine in Ireland, it is the place of my birth and early years. The house at the Old Place was torn down more than half a century ago. The well was filled with rubble to keep anyone that might pass from falling in. All that remains of the house that had been built by my great-grandparents John and Bridget Quinney a few years after they arrived are the crumbling foundations. I return unceasingly to view the ruins and walk the grounds.

Even now you will find late in summer a few apples hanging from the limbs of decaying trees. And at the foot of the gently sloping hill, on a spring evening, the mating calls of frogs can be heard coming from the pond. In winter when the pond is covered with snow, muskrat houses protrude through the ice. When spring comes again, ducks and geese nest and raise their young among the reeds and tall grasses at the edge of the pond. Redwing blackbirds establish their territories, calling from the tops of cattails. Sandhill cranes build their nests at the edge of the marsh. Prairie grasses and forbs and oaks and hickories have been planted on the hill that rises to the east of the Old Place.

When we were young, growing up in the thirties and forties on the farm, my brother and I would look across the field to the Old Place and imagine all the mysteries that must be held by the generations that came before us. With the passing of years, as we moved away and lived our lives in other places, the magic of the Old Place only increased in our imagination. In times of need, as well as in times of ease, I would return to the Old Place to find solace and renewal. I go there regularly now to know that I am an intimate part of the place that is still my home, and to be reminded of the ancestors who have gone before me.

Among the things that were carried up to the farmhouse when our great-aunt Kate died in 1942 were the family photograph albums. The sons and daughters of Bridget and John, and their sons and daughters, made the photographs as they documented their lives at the Old Place and at the farm. A few letters, some diary entries, and a scrapbook of obituaries survive for the historical record. In addition, there are the photographs in albums from my mother's family. And there are the many photographs from albums made by my mother and father as they photographed their young lives, and later after they married, there are the photographs of their early years together. With my birth in the mid-thirties, followed by that of my brother, the years of the growing family were well documented and preserved in family albums.

We — my brother and I — are now the keepers of the farm. Gradually we are converting the farm into sustainable agriculture. Our hope is to make the whole farm into a natural habitat. In the meantime, I photograph the remains of the farm from earlier times. With camera in hand, I make my way to the barn, to the machine shed, to the chicken house, and to the farmhouse, photographing the artifacts of the life that once was here. I go among the ruins and record the afterlife of things. These photographs pay homage to the ancestors that made this place. The past becomes a part of the living present. Lifetimes are burning in every moment.

This place that I continue to write about was made by emigrating ancestors, by ancestors who were born here, and by those who left the place—by all those generations who have been shaped by these few acres of earth and home. These are the ancestors, the generations of old ones, that I have remembered, telling the stories that have been passed to me—stories in words and images that document their lives. There is enough here to know that we are an intimate part of those who have come before us.

Our lives continue—in body, mind, and spirit—from their lives. In this real sense, there is no birth and no death. There is only the one river of life that keeps flowing, and we all are part of it. We know that our ancestors are not merely of a former time. They are with us always, in our daily lives, just as we will be in the lives of those who come after us.

The Old Place

IT MUST HAVE BEEN a morning early in spring, after the melting of winter's snow and the drying of the land by the warming sun, that I formed what would become my first memory. I would have been nearly five years old. Standing beside my father east of the barn, looking to the southeast, we watched as my grandfather, nearing the end of his life, slowly made his way across the field that sloped down to the Old Place. I remember only a dark figure coming toward us. And I remember being startled by my father's comment in the morning air, "Here comes the old man." An old man making his way from an old place: this I would remember.

The Old Place

I have no recollection of my grandfather's arrival at the farm after his perilous journey across the hilly field. He would die within the year, just before the war began. In one of the tattered family albums, my grandfather, John Quinney, appears as a tall, mustached man in overalls standing behind the team of horses and the grain drill in the same field where I would see him later at the end of his life. From my earliest memory to the present moment, my world begins and ends at the Old Place.

My father had been born at the Old Place as the new century began. His would be the last generation to live in the old house. A year after the last aging member of the household, my great-aunt Kate, died in 1942, the house would be torn down. As a boy I would walk across the field and look into the cavity that once was the basement. The ruins of the foundation outlined the house that once rose above and served as a home for three generations of my family.

I don't know when the house was built. It was some years after my great-grandfather—also John Quinney—and my great-grandmother Bridget O'Keefe purchased the few acres in 1868. They had come to the United States on emigration ships from Ireland during the potato famine of the 1840s. They settled in Yonkers, and in 1850 they were married. Whether John and Bridget knew each other before emigrating from Ireland is not known in our family history. We know that in 1859 they moved to Walworth County. After renting an acre or two of land south of Millard, in Sugar Creek Township, they

Grandfather John Quinney in the field at the Old Place in the 1920s

bought the land four miles south that would be the beginning of the farm.

They lived in a small house near the side of the road—where lilac bushes still grow—until building the large frame house a few yards to the south and across the road. The new location overlooked a marsh and a pond. The road curved sharply at the bottom of the hill. Photographs from the early 1900s show scattered outbuildings, an orchard, a well, and the oaks and maples that stand to this day, some as hollow trunks that reach high into the sky and each summer provide nests for red-headed woodpeckers.

Of the next generation, the five children of John and Bridget, some were born in Yonkers and some on the acres south of Millard, before the family moved to the place beside the road that is now called Quinney Road. All grew up at the Old Place and took their turn in the new world. Katherine, the eldest, lived in Chicago part of the time, working as a seamstress and milliner in the house of a wealthy woman named Mrs. Woodward. Thomas and William each married and homesteaded in South Dakota, remaining in or near Alexandria for the rest of their lives. Mary, the youngest, married Henry Reynolds and lived on a farm near Lake Como. John—my grandfather—remained at home and bought more acres and passed the farm on to my father.

My grandfather John married Hattie Reynolds from Rock County in 1894. Then began the third generation to live at the Old Place. Marjorie was the first born, and in her adult life she worked as a maid and owned a roadside tavern, and died of a ruptured appendix at the age of forty. Floyd, my father, was born in 1900, farmed the land, married Alice Marie Holloway, who would become my mother, and died in 1969. Little Nellie, born in 1904, died before she reached the age of two. This was the last generation at the Old Place before it was torn down.

My father and mother built a new house a quarter of a mile to the west where the barn and sheds were located. It is a bungalow-style house, perhaps inspired by my father's trip to California when he was twenty-four. The house was built in the summer of

Great-grandmother Bridget Quinney

Great-aunt Kate Quinney

1930, just in time for the September wedding. I was born in May of 1934, and given the name Earl Richard. My brother Ralph was born two years later. The farm was now our home place. Still, it was the Old Place that held all the mystery we ever needed to know. I sit now on a cement bench near the empty corncrib east of the barn, looking southeast over the sloping field, and gaze longingly at the Old Place.

*T*HE LILACS AND THE SILVER MAPLES—with new shoots and saplings—grow along the old driveway and north of where the house once stood. Rusting fence posts and wire enclose the caved-in well that supplied the needs of three generations. A few apples hang from the branches of what is left of the apple trees. The road at the bottom of the hill is grown over with shrubs and willows. At the pond, frogs croak and chirp each summer night, and in winter muskrat houses rise through the ice and snow. Daylilies grow from the banks of the road that now passes along the south side of the Old Place. For some fleeting moments, I imagine the lives of the ones that once lived here.

The photograph albums provide ample documentation of the Old Place. The center portion of the clapboard house is two storied. On either side are the wings—extending north and south—with an open porch facing east down to the pond. The house is of modest construction and repair. I remember being inside only once; my dad showed me the stairway that he had climbed as a boy each night with a kerosene lamp in hand. In a photograph in one of the old albums, Bridget, in old age, sits in a wicker chair on the sunny side of the house, hollyhocks in bloom.

Marjorie Quinney

On a winter's day, in another photograph, Kate stands in the road at the Old Place and looks toward the farm. Marjorie, in a checkered coat with fur stole, poses behind the Model T Ford—outbuildings in the background. Floyd is in the field south of the house tending to the chickens and cows. Horses and a black and white dog appear in several of the photographs.

Floyd Quinney

There is a photograph of Kate's last year at the Old Place. My father has taken his two sons—Earl and Ralph—down to the house to visit Kate. A very old Kate stands with her sister Mary and visitors from Lake Como. My father is in the foreground as my brother and I pose with Kate. When Kate died the next year, my father came back to the farmhouse before bedtime and told us that Kate had passed away. This is my first memory of a death in the family.

Floyd, Kate, Earl, and Ralph at the Old Place in 1941

Life had finally come to an end at the Old Place. When the house was torn down the next year, my father lamented that Kate's box of buttons had been lost in the destruction. The lament continued the rest of his life.

I have located the original deed and mortgage, dated February 6, 1868, for the purchase of the Old Place. They have been passed from generation to generation, stored in a succession of envelopes and safety boxes. The originals are among the deeds that record the addition of acres that make up the farm.

The documents describe in legal terms the specific location of the thirty acres purchased by John Quinney. The cost of the land is a sum of $300, to be paid in four equal annual payments, with an annual interest of seven percent. No mention is made of a house existing on the property. John and Bridget must have constructed a small house that would serve the family for the first few years.

The mortgage papers contain the signature of my great-grandfather. The lawyer has signed the name John Quinney. On the line is a large X with the lawyer's notation—"his mark." Oh pioneers!

The Three Generations That Lived at the Old Place

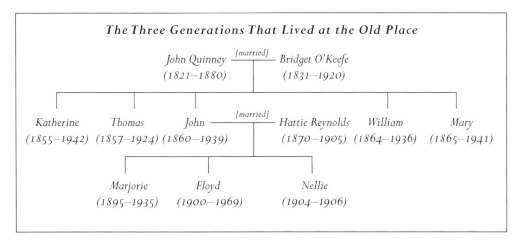

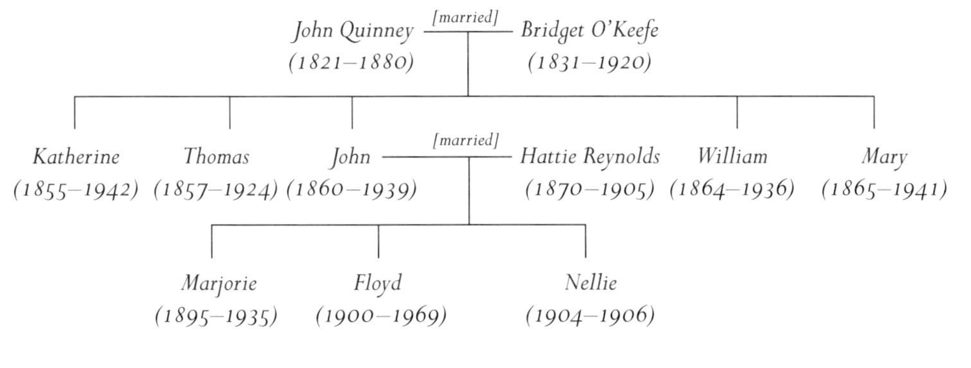

*W*E ARE FAMINE IRISH. This fact was only vaguely recognized as I was growing up. We repeated the litany that John and Bridget had come from County Kilkenny many years ago. That Bridget had smoked a clay pipe. That Kate and Marjorie had worked as seamstresses and maids in the houses and resorts of the rich in Chicago and around Delavan Lake and Lake Geneva. Still, any details about the fleeing of Ireland in the 1840s during the height of the famine were not passed down to us. I have little idea of the difficulties faced by the three generations before me as they assimilated into the culture of the new world. Being famine Irish would have been a disgrace and a stigma on the generations of immigrants. By mid-twentieth century, one could have a sense of pride in being Irish, but one did not connect being Irish with the flight from the great famine in Ireland.

There is one stark piece of evidence that indicates to me that the generations bore a deep scar from being famine Irish. When Kate died in 1942, a few of her possessions were brought up to the farmhouse. They remained in the music cabinet—also from the old house—on the porch for half a century before I took a look at them. Kate had kept a scrapbook for many years of her life, a scrapbook mainly of newspaper clippings of births, marriages, and deaths in the family. But midway in the scrapbook is a leaflet with a colored drawing, a derogatory cartoon about the Irish. An ape-like figure with the tools of a worker poses in Irish coat and top

H.
YOUR OCCUPATION'S GONE.
YOUR job is played out, for they need no more Micks;
Steam-engines now hoist up the mortar and bricks:
Your prospects, I think, are exceedingly blue,
And the only thing left you, in this pinch, to do,
Is to try, on the strength of your mug and your shape,
For a job at the Zoo as some new kind of ape.

Cartoon of the Irish, "Your Occupation's Gone"

hat. The worker has been made obsolete in the course of industrial development. Lines below the figure suggest that the only thing to do is to get a job at the zoo as "some new kind of ape."

You can only guess Kate's reasons for placing the cartoon in the scrapbook. She certainly was recognizing her Irish identity—a lifetime of identification. The message that the Irish are less than human could not be avoided, likely striking a deep chord, and reminding her of the cruel and unfair treatment of the Irish. Such characterization of the Irish could easily cause you to flee from a public identification of being Irish. Just as you had fled from the shame of the great famine.

Although I have tried to trace my Irish roots further back than the famine, searching the national archives in Dublin and the parish records in County Kilkenny, I have failed to learn much about my ancestors before the emigration of John and Bridget. There are bits of information about the possible spellings of "Quinney," variations due to transcriptions of the Gaelic, transpositions at the ports of emigration and immigration, and a possible change in spelling during an early migration from northern to southern Ireland. Quinney may be an Anglicized form of the Gaelic name O Coinne, a descendent of Coinneach. One genealogist that I employed suggested that we descended from a Tyrone O'Quinney who marched with the army of Eoghan Rua O'Neill to the confederation of Kilkenny in the 1640s. The same researcher came to the following conclusion: "It is clear to me that your ancestors belonged to the cotter/labour class, which suffered most as a result of the Great Famine and generally featured in the records as mere statistics." I am assuming this conclusion is the bare fact of my Irish ancestry. A fact that subsequent generations of the family remembered uneasily, and hesitated to pass on to subsequent generations. There was a toll to pay, one that continues to my generation—and perhaps beyond.

The practice of the Catholic religion had dissipated by the time of my father's generation. He would tell of Bridget walking the five miles to attend mass as St. Andrew's Catholic Church in Delavan. Kate, I know, was a devout Catholic. Her black glass rosary rests in a box of trinkets in the attic of the farmhouse. I never heard my father speak about religion in his own life. My brother and I were sent to Sunday school at the Delavan Methodist Church while our parents attended the morning service. Other than always trying to do the right thing, we did not talk about religion at home.

I have always wondered when the Irish accent ceased to be heard among my immigrant ancestors. We would imitate the

Irish brogue on St. Patrick's Day, but never did we think that this was from our original tongue. Did Kate and her brothers and sister speak with an Irish accent? As part of assimilation into the dominant Anglo culture, removing the Irish from your daily speech would be an important thing to do. My guess is that tones and inflections from the old country continued to be heard at the house on the hill. Passing by the Old Place, now, I hear a sound that comes from another land and another time.

I GREW UP ON THE BORDER, and a life has been made from this reality. When it came time for me to recount and to meditate on my life, I titled the book that I wrote *Borderland.* Living on the border, it seems, best describes my personal existence. I might wish that it were otherwise, but a borderland existence it has been from the beginning and, likely, will be to the end.

Being a descendent of emigrants naturally sets the pace for a life. No doubt all emigrants, the generation that left the old country, experienced the pains of entering a new land. They lived their lives never again feeling at home any place in the world. For those attempting a return, even for a visit, a break had occurred that could not be healed. And in the new land, few emigrants ever made a home that they knew for certain would be theirs. Once you leave home, your native land, no matter how tenuous your hold has been, you can never feel at home anywhere you live.

Generations later, the descendents of emigrants are themselves only a step removed from the emigration away from an old place and immigration to a new place. The old country is but a faint memory that has been passed through the generations. Assimilation of the generations into the ways of the new land has all but erased the past, a past that might serve in positive ways to give identity and a sense of being rooted in something. We of the new world forge a life on the borderland.

My world was the world not only of emigrants, but a world of immigrants who continued to be farmers. Five miles away were the small towns of Delavan and Elkhorn. To me these towns were of the other world—streets, brick buildings, offices of doctors and lawyers, churches and schools. I don't think I ever knew a farmer in those years that didn't think that life was better in town. And that people in town were better than they were. Soon I would want to leave the farm to become another person. But I stayed on the border rather than becoming either of the city or the country. I move back and forth between days in the city and days in the country, across the field from the Old Place.

Of course our vision of the urban world—and of the urbane life—was beyond the nearby farm towns of Delavan and Elkhorn. We were in the orbits of Chicago and Milwaukee, each sixty miles away. Our hinterland stretched west of Milwaukee and northwest of Chicago. Kate had commuted to Chicago on the train for years before the turn of the century to work in the house of the wealthy Mrs. Woodward. Marjorie worked in Chicago for some years as well. Walworth County—around Lake Geneva and Delavan Lake—had been the vacation destination of the rich and the rising middle class of Chicago and its suburbs. We of the country regularly came in contact with these strangers. One could not remain completely provincial when there were strangers in our midst.

In the winter we resumed our lives in the country. Except for the occasional trips to Chicago and Milwaukee to see a traveling Broadway musical, to go to a baseball game at Wrigley Field, or to shop and see a movie in an ornate theater on State Street or Wisconsin Avenue. By train or car, the trip to the city was an adventure that would hold us from one time to another. It is a pleasure still to remember my father dressing in his suit, putting on his topcoat and fedora, and heading to Chicago to attend the international stock exhibit. Once he brought home a toy bus for each of us.

In an essay with the title "Something to Write Home About," Seamus Heaney describes the god the Romans called Terminus, the god of boundaries. The Romans kept an image of the god in the Temple of Jupiter on Capitol Hill. An opening to the sky was in the roof above, and as Heaney writes, "as if to say that a god of the boundaries and the borders of the earth needed to have access to the boundless, the whole unlimited height and width and depth of the heavens themselves." Even with boundaries and borders, or especially with boundaries and borders, both gods and humans need to feel that they are unbounded. "A good poem," Heaney adds, "allows you to have your feet on the ground and your head in the air simultaneously." And to this I would add, life itself is both earthbound and open to the spaces beyond. We are simultaneously here and elsewhere. I learned this well on the farm, and down at the Old Place.

ALL THAT I KNOW about the life of my great-aunt Kate could be written in a few lines. Little about her has survived for the telling. One reason for the scarcity of information is the lack of people to pass on thoughts about her. Kate never married, and our families have been small in number. I have found in the top drawer of the buffet at the farm a diary that Kate kept. The diary is for the year 1892, but Kate used the diary over a period of years to record a few brief entries. There is an entry dated 1924 that lists household items; there are a few addresses of relatives; the deaths of her brothers Tom and John are recorded giving the times of death; and she enters the birth of my brother and me. In the entry for my birth, she adds, "A very good looking chap." On the opposite page, in a child's hand that must be mine, my name is scribbled, indicating that I had some contact with Kate, although I do not remember this. Midway in the diary there is a pressed four-leaf clover. We Irish believe, superstitiously, in four-leaf clovers.

Through good fortune the photograph albums that Kate kept, covering a period of nearly forty years, have survived. The albums, with photographs glued to the black pages, were brought up to the farmhouse when Kate died at the Old Place in 1942. Since discovering the albums on the front porch several years ago, I have gone through them with ritualistic regularity. I am the family archaeologist who digs in the buried past to learn about that other time and about those other lives to which I am biologically and psychologically—and spiritually—connected. I am the archaeologist who searches for the artifacts that will shed light on those who came before us. The search—and whatever knowing that may result—is our way of keeping the ancestors with us, as if alive.

Without the stories of those who knew Kate, and without the memories of subsequent generations, I am left to imagine Kate's life from the images in her photograph albums. In the albums that she made during her lifetime, I have a glimpse of her life. Without words to read, or stories to remember, Kate lives in the visual record, as selective as this may be. I study the tattered albums once again. Each time that I sit with them, the world they portray becomes stranger and more complex to me.

There is much information in the albums that will never be retrieved; historians, archivists, and living relatives will never be able to identify many of the people and places that now exist on paper only. The woman in peasant clothing who sits in front of the shed tending her flock of ducks could be in Ireland, or South Dakota, or Wisconsin—certainly a long time ago. There are photos of horses and buggies on streets in small towns somewhere. A tom turkey struts for the hens in a backyard. Waves lap the shore someplace along Lake Michigan. Institutional buildings of brick loom in the distance. Studio portraits of men, women, and children—lost to our memories—gaze at me as I turn the pages. In a meadow beside a creek, the cattle are lowing, and a baby sleeps.

Kate appears often in a fine tailored suit of checkered cloth. She is pictured at the Old Place with outbuildings, marsh, and woods in the background. My dad and Marjorie are in photos at various times in their lives. Bridget is photographed beside the house, a scarf on her head. Large family gatherings are posed on the farmhouse porches. My grandfather John is shocking grain in the field. Kate sits on the edge of an imitation moon—likely from a day at Riverview Park in Chicago. Again in the clothes and the hat that she has fashioned, she stands on the shore of Lake Michigan; a sailing ship is docked in the harbor.

Mary, Kate's sister, appears in numerous photographs in the albums. The youngest of the five children of Bridget and John, Mary married Henry Reynolds in 1881, and moved to the farm at Lake Como. From then on, many of the family gatherings were held at their home. Gatherings are recorded in the photographs taken on the front lawn. Also there are photographs of Mary and Henry spending afternoons at the Old Place. Their children Howard and Birdina are pictured at various stages of their lives. Howard's son Gene, my second cousin, and his wife Betty visit us when we are at the farm. Recently I found Mary's grave in the cemetery at East Delavan.

A motif of farm and city is evident throughout Kate's albums. That she lived part of her life in the city—while simultaneously returning to the Old Place sixty miles to the north of Chicago—is the theme of her life. Twenty-some years ago, I spent several days at the Chicago Historical Society researching the outlines of Kate's life in Chicago. The photograph albums contain many photos of Kate's employer, Anna G. Woodward, widow of Morgan S. and remarried to Emmet B. Thompson, who resided at 414 E. 44TH Street from 1909 to 1916. With the address and Kate's photo albums, I found the building on the corner of E. 44TH and Martin Luther King Boulevard, once named South Parkway. The building, with its stone carvings and cast-iron fence, was just as pictured in the albums. In a photograph in one of the albums, Mrs. Woodward is seated in her stylish electric automobile.

Kate in Chicago on the shore of Lake Michigan

I imagine Kate working at her sewing machine behind the upstairs window. Some days she takes a streetcar uptown to Marshall Field's to shop for material for the making of exquisite dresses and hats. On clear days she walks east to the shore of Lake Michigan before returning to the house of Mrs. Woodward.

Kate put into her albums notices of the high-society adventures of Mrs. Woodward. One newspaper clipping, announcing the marriage of Anna Graham Woodward to Emmet B. Thompson at the Church of Transfiguration, proudly notes: "The bride was in Peking during the Boxer uprising as a guest of Minister Conger, and became known to the diplomatic corps as the 'heroine of the Peking siege.'" Her son, Lieutenant Warren Woodward, who was in the flying service, was killed in France during the war. On another page of the album is a photograph of Mrs. Woodward in a rickshaw, and right below it is a photo of Kate taken at the Old Place. On another page, Mrs. Woodward is seated in her fancy car, parked in front of her building, and right below the photo is a photograph of Kate sitting on the running board of the Model T, crocheting, at

Mrs. Anna Woodward in Chicago

Kate crocheting at the Old Place

the Old Place. It is a day during World War I, and a flag hangs in the front window of the car. At the end of the album is a postcard of the residence of Mrs. Potter Palmer, and an invitation to Mrs. Woodward to attend an afternoon party in the Shakespeare Garden. Also, there are cards of scenes from Ireland that have nothing to do with Mrs. Woodward.

From the probate records at the Walworth County courthouse, I have found that at the time of Kate's death in 1942, her personal estate was $625.37 from cash in the Wisconsin State Bank. Her household furniture was valued at $25.00. She had one-fifth interest in the property and house at the Old Place. I keep Kate's writing desk—a "secretary"—in my living room in town, and someday I will donate her photograph albums to the state archives for safekeeping. Her inkwell, made of iron and green glass, is on my desk providing another day of remembrance and inspiration.

KATE KEPT A SEPARATE ALBUM of newspaper clippings. The cover has the color of a faded rose with a binding that is in threads. I leaf through the album to know more about the events—from birth to death—in the lives of my ancestors. I learn about the things that mattered to Kate.

There are the obituaries clipped from local newspapers, and the obituaries sent to Kate from South Dakota. Bridget's obituary of 1920 is pasted directly to the inside of the front cover. Her grown children survive her: John at the farm, William and Thomas of South Dakota, Mary Reynolds of Lake Geneva, and Kate of Chicago. I had not known that a child had died in infancy shortly after her emigration from Ireland and marriage in Yonkers. Beside Bridget's obituary, Kate pasted a poem with lines that read:

> I did not weep.
> It seemed I did not know
> 'Twas endless sleep.
> And time went on —

> Drab days that groped or sped.
> Somehow I could not learn
> That she was dead.

There are the clippings of the weddings, the births, and the anniversaries. But the reason for the making of the album of clippings is the fact of death, the Grim Reaper. The album is writ large as a cautionary tale that reads *memento mori:* you must die. The obituaries accumulate and accelerate in number. Brother Tom dies in December of 1924; niece Marjorie dies in October of 1935; brother Bill dies in January of 1936; brother John dies in January of 1939; and her sister Mary dies in September of 1941, only a few months before Kate's death. In between are the deaths of young nephews and nieces from infectious diseases and accidents on the highway. From the obituaries I learn about the lives of those who once lived and are remembered in death, in the clippings brittle and fast fading.

Kate followed the fortunes of the hymn "Sweet By and By," which was written in 1865 in Elkhorn, just seven miles east of the Old Place. From the *Chicago Tribune,* Kate pasted the lyrics by S. Fillmore Bennett, with the refrain:

> In the sweet by-and-by,
> We shall meet on the beautiful shore.
> In the sweet by-and-by,
> We shall meet on the beautiful shore.

Later in the album is a clipping about the settlement in an equity court in Boston of the legal rights to the royalties of the hymn. When Joseph P. Webster wrote the music for the hymn, he had signed a contract with Lyon & Healy in Chicago to publish the hymn. After the Chicago fire of 1871, the rights were sold to the Oliver Ditson Company in Boston. The lawsuit in the equity court returned the royalty rights to the Webster estate. Kate's clipping describes the origin of the hymn:

> The origin of the song is interesting: It was written, words and music, in less than an hour and was inspired by a temporary fit of depression of Mr. Webster. It is related that in 1865 Mr. Webster went into the home of his friend, Dr. Samuel F. Bennett, in a most despondent mood. The doctor asked what was the trouble. "It is no matter, it will be all right by and by," was the reply. This remark acted as a flash of inspiration to them both. Dr. Bennett immediately sat down and wrote out the verses and Webster composed the music on his violin. Less than an hour later they were singing the song with two friends.

Joseph Webster continued to teach music in Elkhorn, and wrote the song "Lorena," which became famous after the Civil War. My mother's mother Lorena, as with many young girls of the time, was given the name.

In an article dated March 17, 1937, pasted into Kate's album, President Franklin D. Roosevelt lauds the spirit of St. Patrick. On that day, Roosevelt, delivering a message on the 125TH anniversary of the Hibernian Society of Savannah, Georgia, and the 200TH anniversary of the Charitable Irish Society of Boston, decried that selfishness was the greatest danger confronting the nation, and urged Americans to follow the footsteps of St. Patrick and his epitome of unselfishness. The motto of the Irish societies — "not for ourselves but for others" — may well be "the inspiration for all of us," the President said. Four years later, Kate pasted into her album the article reporting the burial of the President's mother Sara Delano Roosevelt. To the end, Kate's heart was with the Irish and those who supported them.

I sit here at my desk carefully holding in my hands the scissors that Kate used throughout her life of work as a seamstress. The scissors are heavy and large — ten inches in length — and the handles are black. I use the scissors occasionally to cut pages from newspapers of the day. As you may guess, the material things gathered from the Old Place, and the lives imagined of those who once lived there, are the Muses of my life. I need not look farther than the Old Place; it has been my inspiration for a lifetime.

KATE WOULD OCCASIONALLY VISIT TOM AND BILL and their families in South Dakota. I have found in the trunk on the front porch a postcard sent to Kate from Tom. On the front of the card, Tom and his wife Florence are standing in front of their house. On the other side of the card, Tom asks Kate to come out to South Dakota for a visit. A few years later, in the early 1920s, Kate makes the trip, and there is a photograph in her album of Kate and her brothers standing before the camera on a summer's day. The trees are sending shadows across the lawn. Tom will die in 1924, Bill in 1936, and Kate will live another twenty years. They are pleased to be together as they pose for a photograph.

About all I know of Tom and Bill is gleaned from the newspaper clippings saved by Kate and placed in her album. There are other families, I assume, that pass stories about their uncles and

Tom and Florence Quinney in South Dakota

Tom, Kate, and Bill Quinney in South Dakota

aunts, and great-uncles and great-aunts, from one generation to another. I am fortunate to have the obituaries that Kate saved, perhaps with other generations in mind. Obituaries published in newspapers for the public to read are the documents for this family's history.

The headline reads "Thomas H. Quinney called by death." A pioneer of Hanson County, he died at the age of sixty-seven at his home in Alexandria. Tom had traveled to the Dakotas in 1880 to take up a homesteading claim. A year later, he returned to the boyhood farm in Wisconsin and claimed Miss Florence Loomer of Millard as his bride, who survives him. Also surviving is a son, Elwin, Assistant Engineer for the state of South Dakota. A daughter, Lillie May, died in young adulthood of influenza and pneumonia.

Tom's travel to the Dakotas in 1880 to claim a homestead has been described by his son Elwin, and the account has come to me only recently. Starting from Whitewater, a few miles north and west of the Old Place, on February 15TH, Tom and his friend C. H. Nott traveled by rail to Algona, Iowa. Caught in a snowstorm, the train and passengers were blockaded for four days. After shoveling snow, they then pushed on to Emmetsburg. Tom developed back trouble and was forced to lie quietly in a hotel for two weeks. Pressing on by train, the travelers were blocked by snow on their run to Mitchell. Tom and his friend Nott were now discouraged of reaching their destination by rail, and finding their funds running low, decided to walk. Pushing out across the snow-covered prairie, with the white unbroken expanse reflecting painfully the sunlight, their eyes were blinded before they reached Marion Junction. Somehow, the men continued on the next morning groping in darkness in a strange country and without even so much as a trail to follow.

As they struggled on, sustained by hardened snow crust, but suddenly sinking where the tall grass had weakened the crust, Tom and his companion stumbled up the hills and plunged through the ravines, until finally they heard, from a distance, a man calling his cattle. By calls and answers, they succeeded in reaching him and passed the night in his shanty. The next morning, not yet recovered from their snow blindness, they hired the man to lead them to the Barker brothers, who had been old friends of theirs in Wisconsin, and who lived but a few miles away.

As soon as Tom and his friend recovered from the effects of their walk in the snow, they went to Mitchell and filed their homestead claims. After purchasing three dollars' worth of roof boards for their sod shanty, a sack of flour, and a jug of molasses, they took an inventory of cash, and found themselves possessed of just fourteen cents. From here on we are told that Tom obtained a fine property and a comfortable fortune.

The obituary of Tom's death continues: "Death came to Mr. Quinney in the early morning of December 16. He had been ill for several weeks, and for the past two weeks or more it was known by the relatives and friends that his passing was but the question of a short time. He made a valiant struggle against the Grim Reaper, but it was a vain effort, and his never strong constitution was not equal to the struggle." And we are reminded of his accomplishments: "Mr. Quinney was well known and was held in high esteem by a large circle of friends in the county. He served for a number of years as commissioner of Hanson County, having also served as chairman of the board. For a number of years he was president of the Hanson County Agricultural Society, and always had a great interest in the county fair. He was a member of the Alexandria Odd Fellows lodge, and was also affiliated with the local lodge Ancient Order of United Workmen. Mr. Quinney was a good neighbor, a loyal friend, respected by all who knew him." Tom and his family had lived on the farm eight miles south of Alexandria until they moved to town in 1910. Many friends and neighbors were present at the burial at the Green Hill cemetery as the Odd Fellows ritual was conducted.

There is a photograph of Aunt Florence, Tom's wife, in the family album. She is kneeling on the front lawn with her arms around my brother and me. I know that she attended my grandfather's funeral in 1939, her name being in the visitation book. I keep on a shelf of my living room bookcase the copy of *Nursery Rhymes* that she gave to me in 1941 when I was seven, with her inscription "From Aunt Florence Quinney." I remember my father and mother telling me that Florence had told them that one of the great hardships for her when she and Tom were homesteading was keeping rooms clean in the sod house.

A clipping from the Alexandria newspaper, saved by Kate, describes a surprise party for Tom and Florence in 1921 at the time of their fortieth wedding anniversary. The title of the article reads "Mr. and Mrs. T. H. Quinney Victims of Surprise."

> Wednesday of last week was the fortieth wedding anniversary of Mr. and Mrs. T. H. Quinney, and as they were among the real pioneers of Beulah Township, several of their old neighbors of the early days planned a surprise upon the worthy couple. Mr. and Mrs. Quinney were invited to the home of Clifford Shade for supper, and while they were gone the friends made arrangements for the party, and gathered at the home early in the evening, taking care to see that no lights were going about the time the victims were expected to arrive home. The house was filled with old neighbors and friends to the number of seventy when Mr.

> Quinney opened the doors, and when he switched on the lights his face was an index to the great surprise with which he was confronted. He could not say a word for some time, but finally recovered enough to ask if there was anybody in the cellar.
>
> The evening was spent in singing old time songs and talking over the old times down in Beulah Township, in which reminiscing nearly every one of the guests could join. The "gang" had come prepared to enjoy the entire evening, and naturally had not forgotten the "eats," which were excellent and plentiful. It was a late hour when the gathering broke up after presenting Mr. and Mrs. Quinney with a handsome electric table lamp.
>
> Tom has not quite recovered his composure yet, and both he and his estimable wife are still wondering where all the people came from, but both are unanimous in the opinion that the event was a complete surprise, and that they had a mighty enjoyable time.

For William H. Quinney, death came at the age of seventy-two at his home in Alexandria on Monday evening, January 25, 1936, following a stroke from which he never rallied. He had come to Hanson County in 1887, and was united in marriage the same year to Miss Agnes Bamber. Agnes died in 1921, and only two of their five children survived the death of their father. They had homesteaded for some years, and then moved to Alexandria where Bill served as chief of police and night watch for many years. The obituary tells us that he "was possessed of a friendly disposition, and was well liked by all who knew him. He was accommodating to everybody, and was willing at any time to extend aid to those in need to the extent of his ability. As one of the 'old timers' in Alexandria, 'Bill' Quinney will be missed and sincerely mourned by many friends." He is buried in the Catholic cemetery in Alexandria.

In the album, I learn that Agnes, who died fifteen years before Bill of appendicitis and a heart attack, was born in Milwaukee and came to Hanson County with her family in the early 1880s, right after the railroad was built through Alexandria. Her family settled on a claim south of Alexandria, where she lived until her marriage to Bill in 1887. The obituary tells us that "coming from a city to this new life was a great change, but Mrs. Quinney easily adapted herself to pioneer life, and during her later years she took pride in the fact that she was an early settler of Hanson County." The obituary continues: "Mrs. Quinney's life and happiness centered about her family and her home, where she was perfectly happy in contributing to the comfort of her loved ones and her friends. She was of a kindly disposition, friendly towards everyone, and was of a hospitable nature, enjoying the companionship of her friends and neighbors. She was patient, cheerful, and always ready to give help where it was needed."

A postcard in Kate's album illuminates the page. It pictures the cliffs of Dover jutting into the sea. The card is printed in Saxony, by appointment of the King and Queen. The card is dated October 1908, Alexandria. In a beautiful hand, the card is addressed to W. H. Quinney, Delavan—c/o John Quinney. From the note written on the card, I know that Bill has gone back to the Old Place to visit his ailing mother Bridget. Agnes writes to Bill:

> Your postal received. Glad to hear Mother is better. Mary is still very sick so I wish you would come home. You did not acknowledge my letters. Did you not hear from us since you have been there? It seems an age since you left. I hope Mother will get entirely well. But come home as soon as you can. Yours always, Agnes

Bridget would live for another twelve years, dying in 1920. Agnes would die a year later. Bill would live another fifteen years, dying in 1936. "Come home as soon as you can"—Agnes's invitation and plea. It is a call that both beckons us and cautions us to treasure the moments we have now.

Postcard Agnes Quinney sent to Bill in 1908

*H*ATTIE, MY FATHER'S MOTHER, the grandmother I never knew because of her death twenty-nine years before I was born, was always the image I saw in a large oval portrait kept in the trunk on the front porch — the portrait labeled "Floyd's Mother." My father told me the story several times that when she died at the age of thirty-five in 1905, leaving three young children, his father said that he would never marry again because he would never find a woman as good as Hattie.

I have found a studio portrait taken in 1900 in Alexandria, South Dakota, that includes Hattie. In that year, Hattie and John and their children Marjorie and Floyd made the trip to South Dakota, with Bridget, to visit Tom and Florence and their two children. Bridget, in her seventieth year, is in the center of the portrait. John and Hattie are on the right, and the child that would become my father is on his father's knee.

Only recently I have received information—from a cousin in the Reynolds family—that tells me more about Hattie's family of origin, and a few more things about her life. Hattie's great-grandfather, Daniel Reynolds, no relation to the Reynolds family that Mary Quinney would marry into, lived his entire life in Maine and Massachusetts. He fought in the Revolutionary War. He and his wife Thankful, according to records in the National Archives, received a pension after the war. A son of theirs was named Moses, and it was his son Nathan Church Reynolds who migrated to Rock County, Wisconsin. In 1851, Nathan married Mary Potter who had come from Allegany County in New York. Nine children

Portrait of Bridget with the families of Tom and John Quinney in 1900

were born to Nathan and Mary Potter Reynolds, and grew up on a farm near Milton. Until I received the genealogical information, I knew only that Hattie had several sisters and brothers.

The story begins with Seymour, the oldest brother who died in the field at the Old Place. Seymour loved horses and raised colts, and he loved them so much that he used to hug and kiss them. When Hattie died, and John moved across the road to live in Bridget's house, Seymour, always a bachelor, moved into the small house by the lilac bushes. He liked to play cards, and in the winter of 1913, he and some neighbors played until early morning. After the neighbors had left, Seymour found that there was no wood in the house to keep the fire going. He walked to the woods, across the snow-covered field, and fetched a log that he began to carry back to the house. He fell as he stepped on a patch of ice that was covered with snow. He was struck by the log and died. The dog that had accompanied him lay faithfully beside the body for three days, melting the snow to the ground.

Ellen Reynolds was born in 1855. She married William Webb and had four children. She became ill with cancer of the breast, had an operation in Milwaukee, suffered a relapse, and died. Her brother John Reynolds, like his brother Seymour, also loved horses and would bathe them after a day's work in the fields. After a marriage that ended in divorce, he lived in various places and eventually contracted tuberculosis and died in 1907. It is told that his last request was for a stick of candy.

Lucy Reynolds married a man named Ed Dyer and moved to Chicago where he would work in the construction of the World's Columbian Exposition of 1893. Lucy moved back to Walworth County after her husband died, and married a second time. Her sister Anna Reynolds created a long lineage that covers over half of the Reynolds family genealogy. She and her husband, Merritt Baker, moved to Oklahoma because of the offer of cheap land. She moved back to Walworth County after her husband died, remarried, and in her final years tried to make a living crocheting rugs to support herself after her second husband, Dwight Wheelock, died.

Nathan Reynolds, Jr., remained unmarried throughout his life. He suffered from spinal meningitis when young, which left him deaf and unable to talk. The story is told that when he was seven he was struck by lightning while standing by the chimney in the kitchen. In his later years, he was employed as a kitchen helper in the Elkhorn Hospital, and that is where he died.

Alice Mary Reynolds was born in 1869 near Milton. She married Arthur Wheelock from Milton Junction, who would work for the Northwestern and Milwaukee railroads, and then for the Cudahy Brothers Packing Company in Milwaukee. Alice eventually moved to Whitewater, after a divorce, lived alone, and supported herself by taking in washing and ironing. She was finally cared for by a granddaughter, and died in 1958. She was the mother of eight children.

Portrait of the Reynolds sisters

Hattie Reynolds, my grandmother, was born in 1870 on a farm near Milton. Little information is provided about her life in the family genealogy. I know that she moved to the house at the Old Place when she married John Quinney in May of 1894. She died at the age of thirty-five of tuberculosis. Her baby Nellie was one year old, and Floyd was five and Marjorie ten. I take flowers to Hattie's grave at Spring Grove Cemetery in Delavan every spring.

Nellie Reynolds, the youngest of the brothers and sisters, was born in 1873. She was engaged to marry a man of whom her parents did not approve. Her sister Anna had made a blue brocaded silk dress for her wedding, but she died less than two weeks before her seventeenth birthday, and instead of being married in the dress, she was buried in it. Nellie had worked for a woman with six children, and during that time contracted the tuberculosis that caused her death.

A formal studio photograph remains to document the six Reynolds sisters. All are in their finest dresses. Sitting in front, left to right, are Anna, Ellen, and Lucy. Standing in back, left to right, are Hattie, Alice, and Nellie. We of the subsequent generations gaze into the eyes of our ancestors, and hope to know things beyond the few words that have survived.

*M*ARJORIE, AT THE AGE OF TEN, was left without a mother when Hattie died of consumption in 1905. Marjorie's brother Floyd, the boy that would become my father, was five that year. Little Nellie was only a year old. Without a mother, the girls were raised a few miles away in the home of their Aunt Mary Reynolds and Uncle Henry on the farm near Lake Como. Floyd stayed at the Old Place and was raised by his father John and his Aunt Kate. Little information has passed to me about Marjorie's life from her tenth year to adulthood. And the rest of her life is basically a mystery to those of my generation. Whenever I would ask someone who might have known Marjorie or heard about her, the conversation would immediately stop. Or, at most, I would receive an answer such as "Oh, there isn't much to say," or "We didn't know her very well."

I turn to the photo album that Marjorie left when she died in 1935 at the age of forty. Photographs that she took and others that she collected may provide the only remaining window to her life. They allow us, with some imagination, to know about the life that would end abruptly, too soon, from the peritonitis that followed the ruptured appendix.

Floyd and Marjorie at the Old Place, 1903

Portrait of Majorie and Floyd

For years I have kept displayed on the top of my bookcase a framed studio portrait of Marjorie. Her face in soft focus, a string of pearls around her graceful neck, she poses in a dark dress with a delicate lace collar. She looks away from the camera, ever so slightly, lips softly closed in a slight smile.

Fading photographs glued to the black and now brittle pages make up the photo album that Marjorie kept. The album documents the years from about 1900 to the early 1930s. There is a sepia-toned photograph of Marjorie and my father—labeled "Floyd & Myself"—that must have been taken by a traveling photographer. My father appears to be about three and Marjorie about eight. My father is dressed in a skirt and a ruffled blouse, a conventional outfit for an Irish boy, beside a toy wagon. Marjorie is dressed in a stylish long-sleeved dress with her arm resting on a kitchen chair. They are standing in front of the lilac bush. Twenty years later they pose for a photograph taken in a studio in town—a photograph I found recently in a box on the front porch of the farmhouse.

In the album are the photos that Marjorie took of her Uncle Tom and Aunt Florence on a visit to South Dakota. There are many photos of family gatherings at the Old Place and at the Lake Como farm. I pause for a long time to study the photograph of

Front yard at the Henry and Mary Reynolds farm, with Howard, Marjorie, and Henry

the gathering where her Uncle Henry is reaching over her right shoulder and with his right hand is holding her hand in his. Living at her Uncle and Aunt's farm for long periods after her mother died, her Uncle Henry must have been as much of a father to her as her father John. In the background, parked on the lawn, is the ever-present Model T Ford.

I also find the only pictures of my grandfather John as a farmer. He is working in the fields with his horses. The photos

Family gathering at the Reynolds farm, Marjorie and Henry on the left

are labeled "Dad." There are a few photographs of Bridget near the end of her life. And there is Kate dressed in fine dresses at the Old Place and in front of mansions in Chicago and on the shores of Lake Michigan. In another photo, taken from the passenger side of the Model T, the hood ornament rises from the lower corner of the picture as the riders travel down a tree-lined gravel road. I study the buildings and landscapes in the backgrounds of the photographs, and identify some of the places that I continue to see and to think about.

There are the unmarked photographs of people and places

On a road near Delavan, 1920s

Swimming at Delavan Lake

that will remain unknown to future generations. Photographs of soldiers on leave during World War I; photographs of people at picnics beside lakes and rivers; young men and women posing and frolicking in bathing suits. And horses and ponies hitched to carts and wagons; motorcycles in driveways; a biplane parked in a farm field; and dogs running across a snow-covered pond. One could get lost in other times and places.

Midway in Marjorie's album, there are the pages containing the photographs of the man she knew late in her life. His business card is attached—"Lloyd L. Latta, Auto Repairing and Electric Work." The large house of his family, on Highland Avenue in Clinton, appears prominently in pictures of Marjorie and Lloyd posing in various states of composure and abandonment. A few years ago I knocked on the door of the house and was given a tour by the present owner. I learned that Lloyd's sister Ruby, also pictured in the album, was still alive and lived at the top of the street. She died some years ago while I was gathering the courage to ask the questions I would have liked to ask.

Lloyd Latta and Marjorie at the Latta house in Clinton

The silence that inevitably followed any of the inquiries I made about Marjorie no doubt came from the fact that she was a single woman, who for the last part of her life owned and operated a tavern. While other women in the area during the twenties and thirties were marrying farmers or teaching in country schools, Marjorie was taking another direction. Her life caused in others both fascination and condemnation. Marjorie has been the woman of mystery all my life.

Before operating the tavern known as The Shingle Inn, located on Highway 14, five miles south of Delavan, Marjorie worked as a maid at the Delavan Inlet Inn and at the Wisconsin School for the Deaf in Delavan.

Marjorie at the Old Place

I assume that she lived in the house at the Old Place with her father and Aunt Kate a good part of the time during those years. The Shingle Inn, which she owned in partnership with Joseph McCabe, had served as a bootlegging operation during Prohibition. The inn still exists, now as a "gentlemen's club" featuring dancing girls, and I pause each time I pass by.

Twenty years ago I went to the Walworth County Court House in Elkhorn to look at the probate records that were filed after Marjorie's death on October 31, 1935. The heirs to the Estate were John Quinney and Floyd Quinney. The Personal Estate was listed:

Cash, State Bank of Elkhorn	$351.50
Cash, Citizen's Bank of Delavan	41.73
Trust Certificate, Citizen's Bank	187.83
Cash on hand	35.00
Ford Coupe, 1930 model	60.00

Marjorie's one-half portion of The Shingle Inn at the time of her death was noted with the listing and value of various items, including liquor, tobacco and cigarettes, candy and nuts, glassware, two tables and six chairs, radio, cabin, three beds and springs, and a cash register.

PERIODICALLY — OUT OF NEED IT SEEMS — I page through the photograph albums that survived the destruction of the Old Place for glimpses of my father's life when he was a young man. Outside of the childhood photograph of him with Marjorie, standing beside the lilac bush, the photos begin when he is in his teens. Sometimes he is pictured in the work clothes of a farmer, and other times he is dressed in a suit, shirt, and tie and wears a fedora hat. He is pictured with aunts and uncles, with other people of his age engaged in various activities, and there are the many photos of him in or near his Model T Ford. I favor, especially, the photographs of him working with horses in the field or hauling cans of milk to the factory in town. After finishing the eighth grade, rather than going to high school, he stayed at home to help his father with the farm work.

Two items from my father's life I keep close to me. One is the small oil lamp that he carried nightly as a boy up to his bedroom in the house at the Old Place. He often told me about going up the dark and narrow stairway with the light of the lamp. I keep the lamp on the buffet in the dining room of the house at the farm.

The other artifact — from the archaeology of my father's life — is the camera that he owned and used for many of the photos that appear in the family albums. The camera has a bellows that folds out and is held at the waist for the taking of fine pictures. It is a Kodak Autographic, and I keep it in the middle drawer of the chest beside my writing desk. This is the camera that he took with him when he traveled west to California.

Several years ago I found in the music cabinet on the front porch of the farmhouse the cards and letters that my father had written to Kate and Marjorie during the trip to California. After the harvest was completed in September of 1924, he and his good friend Mervin Kittleson began the cross-country trip in the Model T Ford. Parts of the Lincoln Highway had been completed, and other parts were in stages of construction. They stayed in California for the winter, working at restaurants and on the towers for the electric power lines. They returned home in time for the planting of crops in the spring. In the packet of cards and letters that Kate and Marjorie had saved were the negatives for the photographs that my father had taken on the trip. They had survived the heat and the cold of sixty-five years on the front porch.

The travelers departed from the driveway of the Kittleson farm on the morning of September 16TH. By nightfall they had reached Clinton, Iowa. My father immediately wrote a postcard to Kate: "Arrived here at Clinton, Iowa at six o'clock. Are spending the night at the tourist camp. Have just gone over the Mississippi River. Had three flat tires, but didn't have to buy any new ones." Five days later, upon arriving in Laramie, Wyoming, he writes to Marjorie about the hills and the boulders, the pine trees, and the snow on the mountains. He concludes the letter:

Mervin Kittleson and Floyd beginning the trip to California, 1924

"We meet cars from every state on the Lincoln Highway. Lots of tourists at the tourist camp. We use our pillows twenty-four hours each day. Sleep on them at night. Sit on them all day. We intend to get to Salt Lake City in about three days but you won't have time to write us there. And we don't know which trail we will take from there. But in case of sickness or anything like that a telegram would find us at the tourist camp. Had a chance to get a job with a threshing gang. Will close and make our bed. As ever, your brother."

They arrive in San Francisco on October 3RD. Writing to Kate, my father notes that thus far the cost for the trip is $52 each, including all auto expenses, eats, groceries, and camp fees. "A slow rain all day. Jobs seem scarce around this city. If we don't find work here we will start for Los Angeles." Later in the week they arrive in Los Angeles, and my father writes to Marjorie: "Got to Los Angeles at noon. Reminds me of Chicago. Buildings sixteen to twenty stories high and people galore. Came through Hollywood on our way here. Nice city with fine homes with pretty flowers and big palm trees. Surely a rich man's city."

They continue to explore that city and the towns along the beach. They attend services at a Methodist church, play pool, go to the movies, attend a concert in the park, swim in the ocean, rent a two-room cottage in Huntington Park, and find jobs in a restaurant. My father tells Marjorie: "There is an Irishman working with us by the name of Jack Brett. He is twenty-eight years old. Has been in this country ten years but has the Irish brogue. Keeps us laughing most of the time." By the end of October they are working for the power company putting in forms and pouring concrete. Eventually they will be climbing the high towers and receiving 95 cents an hour.

In the letters, my father often inquires about his father and the work at home. "How is pa coming with the work? Does he still go to the corner with the milk? Suppose the nights are getting chilly now. Are the potatoes dug and how are they?" Later he asks about the trading of the drakes, the gander, and the gobbler, and suggests that four hen turkeys ought to be kept. He adds, "If

Seal Beach

Long Beach

the Ford starts hard there is a five gallon can of winter cylinder oil upstairs in the granary. Suppose it keeps pa pretty busy doing chores now. Hope you are all well."

At Christmastime my father receives in the mail a necktie from Kate and a shirt from Marjorie. "Many thanks to both of you for remembering me." From a girlfriend in Delavan he receives a box of six handkerchiefs, initialed. As the new year begins, the rains have come and water is up to the cottage door, and seals swim up to the beach. My father is beginning to think about buying a suitcase for when he will have to pack and return home. "The old one is pretty well shot."

The last week of February my father writes to Marjorie to tell her about the boat trip that he and Mervin have taken to Catalina Island. From the deck of the boat Avalon he has taken photographs: "And if they are good will send some home. There were over 500 passengers on the boat. Saw a whale come to the top and gush water in the air three times then disappeared. After we reached Catalina Island we took a ride on the glass bottom boat. Just wonderful to see animal and plant life in the ocean. Could look down in the water to the depth of 75 feet seeing the different kinds of fish, clams and weeds." He then tells Marjorie, "Each of us bought a souvenir, an abalone shell." A short time ago, I found the iridescent abalone shell in a box in the attic of the farmhouse. The shell now sits prominently on the shelf of the corner cabinet in the great room of my house in the city.

On the Avalon to Catalina Island

Early in March my father writes Marjorie that he has received her letter, "and as dad says to come home will work until March 11TH." He asks if the feed is holding out. And in a letter to Kate, he tells her that he has purchased his ticket to travel home on the Southern Pacific, and that he will arrive in Chicago at seven o'clock in the morning, Thursday, March 26TH, and that he will probably get to Delavan on the one o'clock train. He adds: "I bought a black genuine cowhide suitcase and it won't be a bit too big for all I have to put in it."

In the days remaining, before leaving California, my dad and Mervin went to Riverside, San Diego, and Tijuana, Mexico. They picked up their mail for the final time at the post office in Seal

Beach. The last letter home ends: "Could plainly see the snow capped mountains from here Sunday morning which are 50 to 60 miles away. According to the papers eight inches of snow fell in the mountains Saturday, but the weather here was just like spring. No snow. Just a little shower of rain. Guess this is all for this time. Floyd."

Floyd photographed by Marjorie, Delavan, 1926

Back in Wisconsin, the crops were planted in the spring of 1925, tilled in the summer, and harvested in the fall. Seasons came and passed, and my father met my mother at a dance in Delavan on a Saturday night in the fall of 1929. They were married the next year in September. I was born on a day in May in 1934, and my brother was born two years later. Mervin farmed for the rest of his life a few miles to the north. Occasionally he came to the house for a visit.

In a gray metal box, I have a few letters that my father wrote to me after I left home. I read them occasionally, when I have the need to hear his voice. And I look longingly at the photographs that he took during the trip of his lifetime. This is just dandy—a word that my father often used in his letters—with me.

Emigrants and Pioneers

*M*Y FATHER RETURNED from his trip to California in March of 1925 in time for spring planting. He took over the responsibilities of the farm from his father upon returning from California. Four years later, in 1929, on a Saturday night in a dancehall above a store on the main street of Delavan, he met Alice Marie Holloway, and they were married in September of the following year. I was born four years later, followed in two years by the birth of my brother.

The marriage of my father and mother brought the history of other families to the farm. Joined to the families Quinney, O'Keefe, and Reynolds, were the families Holloway, Bray, Wishart, and Taylor. Emigrating from England about the same time as the Irish emigrated, these families settled in the communities a few miles north of the Old Place, in the pioneering settlements of Millard and LaGrange. Through several generations, families and marriages culminated in the marriage of Alice Holloway and Floyd Quinney.

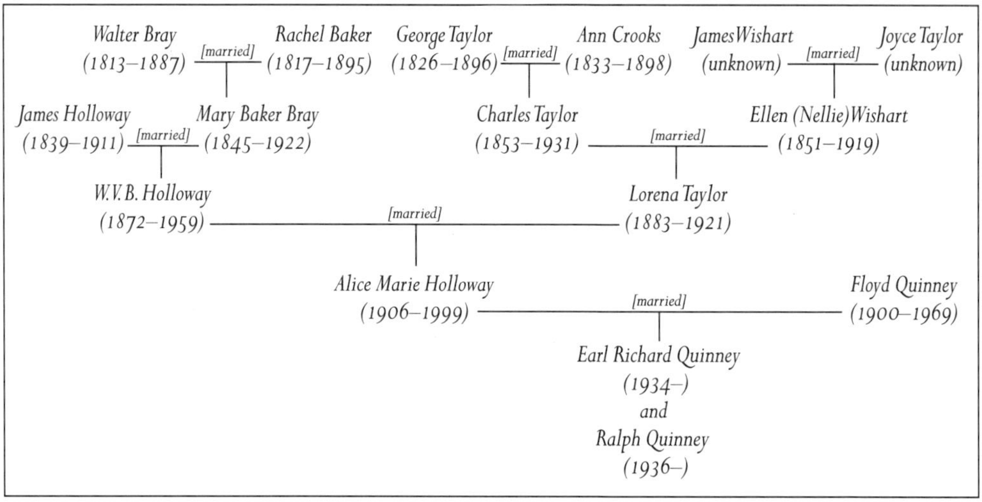

A SMALL, SPARE DIARY remains from the ocean voyage of my mother's grandfather James Holloway to the new world. He departed from Liverpool on the S.S. Damascus in August of 1865 with the words "To America." On the ship's passenger list, his age is given as twenty-six, and his occupation as farmer. On board he writes: "Very rough—we were very ill." "The waves keep dashing over her boughs." Later in the voyage, on a Sunday: "The weather was very fine, the sea was smooth as a pond." Leaving the family farm in West Buckland in North Devon, James had purchased a ticket for passage to Australia, but changed his mind at the last minute, and booked passage to Quebec. He arrived at the port in Quebec on September 20TH, after the voyage of thirty days. From Canada he made his way to Walworth County, Wisconsin.

James Holloway packed a copy of the *West Buckland Year Book* when he sailed from England. I have found the book in the emigration trunk now stored on the front porch of the farmhouse. In the book is a poem directed to the "Emigrants," to all those who will leave the old country for a life in the new world. The first stanza reads:

> I've seen a mother weeping, because her son must roam,
> To seek his fate and fortune, far from his childhood's home;
> I've heard a father groaning, when the daughter of his love

Hath left the parent hearth, another's tenderness to prove.
And well, methinks, Old England, such grief beseemeth thee,
When so many sons and daughters seek a home beyond the sea.
Oh! Had it but been granted by a wise directing Hand,
That one and all could plenty find within their native land;
If intercourse of "near and dear" might last till death unbroken,
That last sad word of parted friends remains a word not spoken;
If families were not dispersed, and home not rent asunder,
Men would not dream of Paradise as some unearthly wonder.

Generations later, we sons and daughters of sons and daughters seek our own good fortunes. And we dream of a paradise that cannot be found in this earthly existence. Daily we live as emigrants from another land.

Tales of virgin lands, of limitless acres that could be acquired for a song, lured the sons and daughters from the failing farms in the west of England. Soon after his arrival, James met Mary Bray, who had come from Devon in 1867 with her father and mother, Walter Bray and Rachel Baker Bray, and brothers and

Walter Bray

Rachel Baker Bray

Portrait of James and Mary Bray Holloway with Lizzie and Will

sisters on the ship Nova Scotia. They would marry, have two children, Will and Lizzie, and move several times from one farm to another. James died in 1911, and Mary in 1922. James was remembered in an obituary as "a devoted husband, a loving father, a kind and helpful neighbor, ever ready to do a kindly act." He held offices in the county, and was regarded as a successful farmer. Will—known by his initials W. V. B.—eventually became father to my mother, Alice Marie, and would be my grandfather.

WILL HOLLOWAY married Lorena Taylor in 1903. The Taylors had started emigrating from Yorkshire in the late 1830s. Conditions in American were better than those in England for the laboring class. One of Lorena's ancestors, Joshua Taylor, Jr., already in the new world, wrote back to his brother and sisters as they were preparing to emigrate: "I am very glad you have made up your mind to come to America. I think it will be the best move you ever made in your life. It is a foolish idea that some people get into their heads there is no place like Old England, for this is a better country than England has ever been in your days or ever will be." The letter offers advice for the voyage and a list of provisions needed for starting the new life in Wisconsin.

George Taylor, my mother's maternal great-grandfather, was a cabinetmaker and carpenter who emigrated from England

George Taylor

Ann Crooks Taylor

in 1851 with his bride Ann Crooks. George designed and built several handsome Greek revival farmhouses that still stand in LaGrange Township. One of their sons, Charles H. Taylor, married Nellie Wishart in 1876. They farmed successfully on Territorial Road, and one of their children, Lorena, would become my mother's mother after marrying Will Holloway.

Wedding portrait of W. V. B. (Will) Holloway and Lorena Taylor Holloway

My MOTHER often pointed out to me the wooded place, located on Tamarack Road, where once stood the house that her grandmother Nellie had lived as a child in the large household of the Wisharts. James Wishart had sailed from England in 1827. His parents, John and Ann Wishart, who were of Scottish birth, soon followed him. Sailing at the same time, and on the same ship, with her family, was the woman who would become his wife in 1833, Joyce Taylor. They lived for a few years with their families in the state of New York, and in 1844 they sailed west by way of the Great Lakes. Landing in Milwaukee, they traveled by team and wagon the forty miles to LaGrange. James had apprenticed to the trade of blacksmithing before emigrating, and he continued blacksmithing until he died in the early 1880s. Fading portraits, passed through the generations, remain of the many Wisharts and Taylors. Identifications are not always certain as time passes and ancestors are forgotten.

Alice Marie Holloway

As the only child of Will and Lorena Taylor Holloway, and the great-granddaughter of James and Joyce Wishart and George and Ann Taylor, my mother was born in 1906 on the farm north of Millard. When she was fifteen, her mother Lorena died of Bright's disease at the age of thirty-eight. Three years later her father married Mabel Stiles. My mother kept a framed portrait of her mother throughout her life. The portrait was on the table beside her chair when she died in 1999, just before her ninety-third year.

My mother began keeping a diary in 1916 when she was nine years old. She made an entry every day for five years. With a coupon clipped from a box of cereal, my mother had ordered a camera, and it arrived on the 25TH of March, 1916. She wrote in her diary for that day: "Hunted eggs all day. I got 2 eggs for myself and 30 for mama. Played in the mud with ma's boots on. Papa went to town. I got my Kodak." On May 4TH, just after her tenth birthday, she wrote:

> I took my camera to school. Teacher showed me how to take a picture. Teacher took a picture of me. Jack (my cat) would not hold still so I could not take his picture. We went to Millard and back in the car. I wore my hat to school.

And on May 7TH:

> We had a short auto ride. Took Grandma's picture. I had the head ache all day. Papa and I went to the woods. I took a picture of mama and papa in the car. Papa took a picture of me at night.

Will and Lorena Holloway, photographed by Alice, 1916

The photographs mentioned in the diary are in the album that my mother kept when she was young and growing up on the farm. When I look at the photographs, I know that the camera was a way of exploring the world and recording the experiences of everyday life. A way of knowing that there is order in the universe, and that all may be well.

The Farm

ALICE AND FLOYD had spent a Sunday afternoon in 1930 at Whitewater Lake. They were dressed in their best clothes. Cows were grazing on the hill that sloped to the water. Alice took a picture of Floyd, hat in his hand. On the back of the photograph, she wrote: "A happy day we spent at Whitewater Lake, June 1930. At nite we went to the show at Delavan. The nite I gave Floyd 'the answer'." In the album that I now have, there is the photograph of her standing in the park overlooking Lake Michigan. On the back of the photograph, she wrote: "Taken in Milwaukee the day after Floyd gave me my engagement ring. Went to Kenosha, Racine and Milwaukee. Had dinner in Kenosha. Called on Kelloggs in Milwaukee and went to a show. A very happy day." This is the ring that I have placed in a box for safe keeping, in a box that also contains the wedding ring that my mother gave my father the day they were married.

My mother was twenty-four when she married my father, and he was thirty. They each had a few years of living separate adult lives before meeting each other. He farmed the land and hauled

Floyd at Whitewater Lake, June 1930

Alice in Milwaukee, June 1930

milk to the dairy in Delavan. In his album of this period, he is shown at work and at gatherings with friends, some who are surely his girlfriends. In the album that she kept, there are photographs of parties with her friends, outings with Elma and Thelma Olsen, and an excursion to Starved Rock along the Illinois River.

Wedding day, Floyd and Alice, September 15, 1930

Mabel Stiles Holloway and Will Holloway

Late in her life she would tell about the trip to Starved Rock with her girlfriends.

Inspired, no doubt, by the houses he saw in California, my father built a bungalow-style house at the farm. It was ready to be occupied when my mother and father married in September of 1930. The wedding was held at the house of her father and stepmother in Millard. They took photographs to record the day. The framed photo of the newlyweds was placed on the dresser in their bedroom, where it stood for nearly forty years. They are posing in the driveway, just before getting into the Chevrolet to begin the honeymoon that will take them on a week's trip to Niagara Falls and back through Windsor, Detroit, and Chicago. The honeymoon is documented in an album of the photographs that they took along the way.

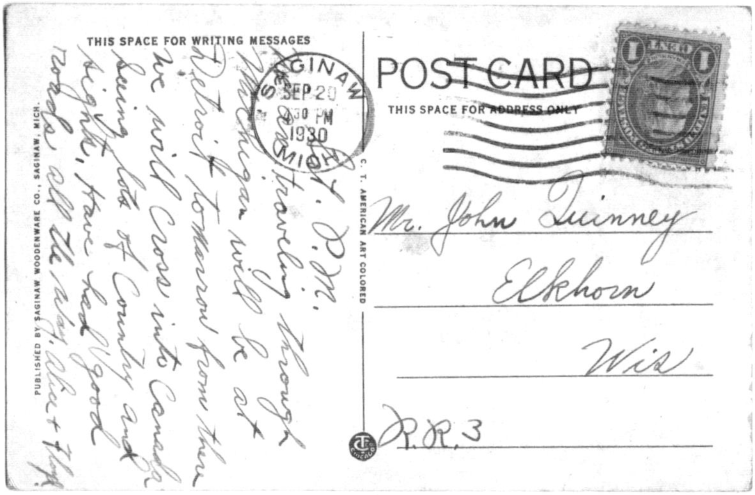

Postcard from the honeymoon

THE NEWLY MARRIED COUPLE settled into the new house on the farm immediately upon returning from their honeymoon. They must have kept a close watch on the Old Place as John and Kate were living the last decade of their lives. But the photographs that follow the wedding and the honeymoon are of the new life at the farm. They took photographs of the new house and of work around the farm. With the birth of their first son in 1934, and with the birth of their second son two years later, the years from the mid-thirties to the early fifties are as fully documented as life can be with the aid of a camera.

How pleased my parents were with my birth. I am placed in all my nakedness on the kitchen table that has been moved to the back porch where the morning sun shines through the tall windows. On my stomach, face turned to the light, I cast an eye to the world. Throughout the year they hold me as the camera records our collective existence. Sometimes my father is in his overalls and other times he is dressed for a Sunday outing. In the snow of winter, or on a summer day, we prepare for a ride in the car. And there I am in the ubiquitous egg crate that serves as my carrier. On my first birthday, with my cake of one candle, I am placed in the south window. Never was there a baby cared for as this one.

Held by my father

Held by my mother

Christmas day, 1934

Sometime ago I removed one of the photos from the album and continue to keep it in a frame on my dresser. My father

My first birthday

has placed me on top of some straw that fills the wheelbarrow. He is pushing the load through the snow between the milkhouse and the back door of the house. My mother has come out to photograph the occasion on this winter's day. On the same day, in my snowsuit, I am playing in the barnyard. Later I stand in front of the decorated Christmas tree that has been placed on the front porch to receive the available light. What a day that was.

In the wheelbarrow

Brothers, 1936

The album ends with the birth of my brother Ralph. In one of the first photographs of that time, our dad is sitting on the porch holding the two of us—and I am looking worried. Next to this picture is a photo of me sitting close to the cat on the sill of the basement window. Soon I will be playfully nudging my brother as he lies on the card table for his picture in the sun. A new album will be needed to record the rest of our growing years, from the late thirties to the end of the war years.

With my mother and brother Ralph

A photograph that I have taken from the album, and placed in a frame on my desk, is of me at the age of three on the seat of the horse-drawn grain binder in the field north of the house. On the back of the photo, my mother has written this: "Our new grain binder, 1937. Cutting grain on our very own land. How Earl loved to ride." This photograph is an early sign that I would

On the grain binder, 1937

be working long and hard days in the fields, often not to my liking. But a sign also of the attention and care that would always be given to me—on the farm, and all the time away from it.

Hauling firewood

Ralph watering the Jerseys

I LOOK AT THE PHOTOGRAPHS taken during the five years between 1936 and 1941, and I see the young and formative years of the two brothers, Earl and Ralph. Beyond the fascination of seeing these two boys early in life, I recognize the great attention that their parents are giving them. I count 170 photographs placed in the albums for this period, more photographs than for any other period in the life and times of this family. Clearly this was a time filled with new life, a time when my mother and father were most interested in recording our lives on film. With the Kodak box camera, they took turns photographing the pleasures of their daily lives. In retrospect, we who remain could weep for what has been lost—the lives of our parents, foremost. And we could, and we do, give our thanks for the good fortune of this family.

The photographs, and the making of the photographs, were not meant to show or comment on the larger social and economic conditions of the late thirties and early forties. These were the Depression years. The family farm, at least in southern Wisconsin, was still based on a subsistence economy. A team of horses drew the field equipment. Feed—oats, corn, and hay—for the small herd of milking cows was grown entirely in the fields of the farm. Other animals—chickens, sheep, and pigs—were raised mainly for use on the farm, and any surplus, especially eggs, was traded for groceries at the end of the week. At year's end, with the filing of income tax, little or no profit could be noted. Simply getting by was the order of the day, but getting by was all that was needed.

My awareness of an outside world, in addition to anything I might hear from the conversations of adults, came from listening to WLS radio from Chicago. I remember the daily stock reports, heard either in the barn during milking time or in the house at noon or at suppertime. I remember well my grandfather Holloway arguing good-naturedly on Saturday nights about Roosevelt's New Deal. I thought, as much as I could think then about such matters, that the Democratic ideals of Julius Johnson, my grandfather's brother-in-law, were the right ones. The night would end with popcorn for everyone.

THE WILD WEST was in our imaginations as we were growing up in Wisconsin in the 1940s. We always had horses to saddle and to ride, sometimes saddling the large workhorses. Ralph and I would listen to the latest adventure of The Lone Ranger on the radio in the late afternoon, and then ride our horses reenacting the adventures of the Lone Ranger and Tonto. On summer evenings, I rode to the end of the pasture to round up the herd of cows for milking back at the barn. Each morning, before sunrise, while doing the chores, we would turn on the radio to hear country music from Chicago's WLS. Sometimes on a clear Saturday night, we could hear The Grand Ole Opry from Nashville.

I thought of myself as a cowboy. Whether in play or work, or in times of trouble, I donned my cowboy clothes and faced the challenge. One Saturday morning when I was six, I dressed in jeans and cowboy shirt, placed a bandana around my neck, fastened a holster to my belt, and drove with my parents and brother to the Delavan Clinic to have my tonsils and adenoids removed, under ether. My lariat was always hanging on the coat rack on the back porch, ready to be taken down and to accompany me on the next adventure.

My cowboy life was observed and encouraged by others. I keep three postcards on my desk to this day. One card is a publicity photo of Roy Rogers sent to me by my great-aunt and great-uncle, Tom and Myra Gregg, mailed during their trip to Los Angeles in 1940. Miss Roeker, my first grade teacher at Dunham School, sent me a postcard of "Greetings from Mexico" with a photo of a small boy in a Mexican hat leaning against a sycamore tree and strumming a small guitar.

Dr. Rolland Anderson—our veterinarian for cows, horses, sheep, and pigs—sent a postcard from a trip to Cheyenne, dated March 16, 1946. The card has a drawing of a cowboy herding cattle on the range, and a poem that ends as follows:

> For a kingly crown in the noisy town
> His saddle he wouldn't change—
> No life so free as the life we see,
> Way out on the cattle range.

Dr. Anderson wrote a note to "Dear Floyd & Family" on the reverse side: "I am on my way to Colorado and waiting in Cheyenne so I thought I'd send this card to the boys. Time to go. Yours truly, Rolland Anderson." Upon his return, he brought me a fine lariat and taught me how to rope. The lariat with its brass honda hangs above my desk as I continue to do my daily work.

Mamas, let your babies grow up to be cowboys.

I ONCE READ A LETTER written by John Steinbeck where he said that being seated at his writing desk was similar to mounting the seat of a horse-drawn wagon. Each morning he would approach his desk, climb into the seat, take hold of the reins, and ride off for a morning of travel. Since reading the letter, I have thought of myself doing the same thing each morning. My own early life of mounting the seat of the horse-drawn grain binder, or the seat of the Oliver tractor for a day of work, was a similar journey of the imagination. My writing—my need to write—goes back to an earlier life.

Except for the steady drone of the tractor, I would be in the silence and solitude of a full day under the big sky. There was the peace that comes with

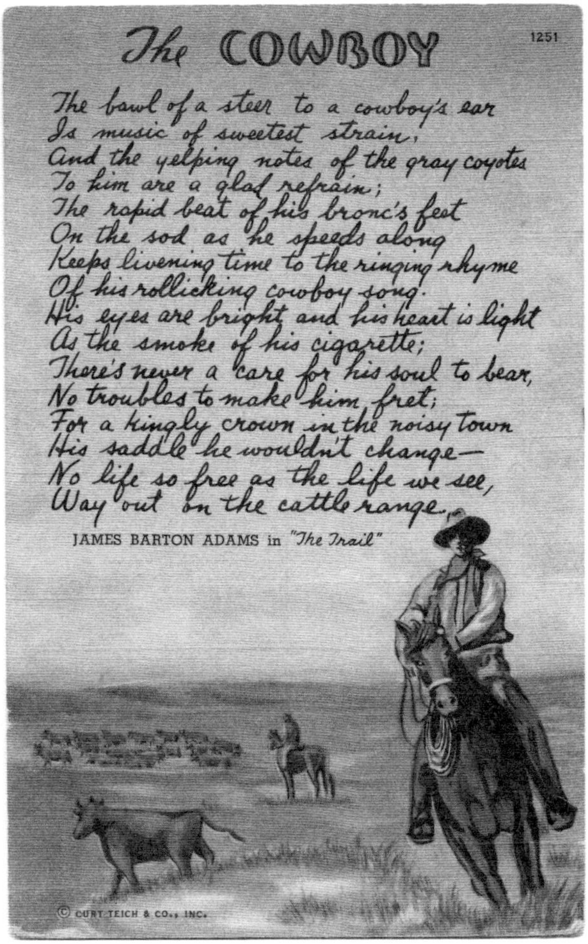

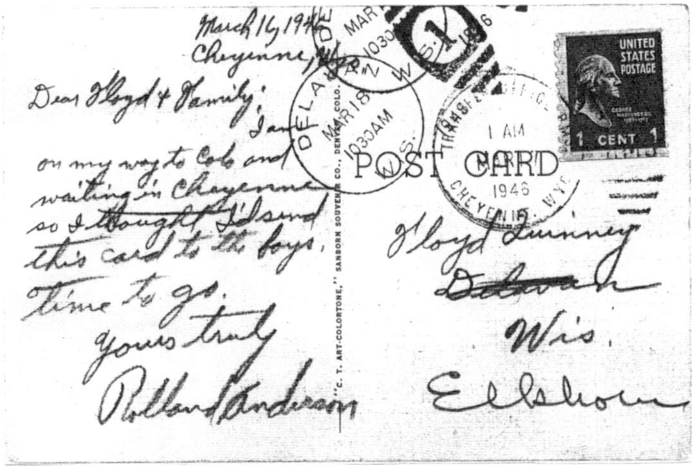

Cowboy postcard from Dr. Anderson, 1941

concentration on the task at hand—guiding the tractor between the rows of corn as I cultivated the land. Dream-like thoughts would come for brief times, and then disappear as I was brought back to attention. Such work has provided a model for a lifetime.

Hard work on the farm afforded a minimum of time for reading anything other than the landscape. I find a few children's books in the attic boxes, books of nursery rhymes, bird identification, and the Indian tribes of Wisconsin. Three books do stand out in my memory of childhood. One is *Hurlbut's Story of the Bible* given to me by my Uncle Lloyd and Aunt Elsie, Christmas of 1943. Another is *The Rover Boys at School,* a book that I would ask my mother to read to me at bedtime. The other is *The Adventures of Huckleberry Finn* given to me by my mother and father in December of 1943 when I was nine. To this day, these three books are prominently displayed in my bookcase. They represent a literary heritage that seemed rich enough to me at the time.

My mother had taught the eight grades for five years at Bay Hill School before she was married. She had completed the nine months of rural education courses at Whitewater State Normal School. Upon marriage, her career in teaching was automatically ended by state law. I sensed that my brother and I had become her students.

My father finished the eighth grade at Dunham School—the school that I would also attend, within walking distance of the farm. Needed on the farm by his father, his education was completed by his early teens. But his love of poetry—learned and recited at school—continued throughout his life. I would be both surprised and enchanted each fall, as we picked ears of corn in the field, when he would joyfully begin to recite, "The golden rod is yellow; the corn is turning brown; the trees in apple orchards with fruit are bending down." The intertwining of poetry and farming has tied me to the farm—as well as to poetry—for life.

I have always had the need to write, to express myself in writing. I have also had the need to photograph, to compose and capture in an image that which is beyond the words of everyday discourse. One finds the means at hand to give substance and meaning to this daily existence.

Occasionally I will examine the photograph albums for an image of the life that once was at the farm and at the Old Place. Sometimes I write a few words about the lives of my ancestors. To remember them—and to gain some understanding of where I began and who I am. And where I might be going.

First day of school, September 1940

ON THE FIRST DAY OF SCHOOL, the day after Labor Day, our mother without fail would take a photograph of our departure. Ralph and I would be dressed appropriately—usually in our overalls—and we would have our notebooks and lunch pails in hand or in our bags. We might be standing beside our bicycles ready to mount and take to the road that would take us the mile and a half to Dunham School. I sang exuberantly "Oh what a beautiful morning" as we pedaled out of the driveway and headed down the gravel road.

We were photographed through the seasons of the year. We posed with our dogs, puppies, cats and kittens, calves, and chickens. Our pictures were taken as we worked in the fields with the horses and on the tractor. Photographs were taken each year during the threshing of the oats. And I remember well the day that

Threshing day

Grain wagon

With corn knives and scythe

we all drove the pickup truck down to the woods to make fence repairs and deposit refuse in the ravine that served as the local dump. We packed a lunch for the trip.

Several photographs in the album record the day that Ralph and I first cut grain alone. In July of 1944, I am ten, as mother noted on the back of the photo, and Ralph is eight. Dad stands beside us as I drive the tractor and Ralph releases bundles from the binder. Do I remember that day, or is it the memory of looking at this photograph for nearly sixty years that remains in my mind? Either way, I know what is real. And it is the same with the scenes where our mother recorded Ralph mowing hay with the horses, and the day that I began to cultivate corn in the field west of the house.

THE PERSON that I would become was nurtured during the years of the war and the transformation of the family farm. At Dunham School we were given the *Weekly Reader,* and I learned about the battles being fought in countries far away. Photographs of Dwight D. Eisenhower and other heroes of the war appeared on the front page each week. Meanwhile, we collected the specimens of nature and placed them in the museum cabinet along the back wall of the one room that served all eight grades. Radio programs of instruction in art, music, and natural history came daily from WHA, the state's educational station in Madison. After a day of play and the learning of new things, we walked home for an evening of chores. On Sundays, our parents made certain that we went to Sunday school at the Delavan Methodist Church.

Grain binder and tractor, 1944

Ralph mowing hay, 1947

Cultivating corn, 1947

In retrospect, I wonder about the particular sense of the religious—of spirituality—that I was developing during those years of the 1940s, from first grade to the beginning of high school. I don't remember ever talking about religion at home. There were Bibles on the shelf, but they were not consulted or read. At bedtime, I might ask my mother to read a story from the Bible, but would be offered instead another chapter of *The Rover Boys at School.* Yet I observed a deep and unspoken spirituality in both of my parents. The verbal instructions were goldenly simple: do unto others as you would have them do unto you.

To this day when I am asked to define religion I give an answer that is focused on individual experience. Religion is to be found inside of the self, not in an organization or in rituals and theologies. The spirit moves, especially, in times and places of solitude. And anything that can be called "divine" is located within me in the course of everyday life.

The notion of a theistic being or force beyond human existence is outside of the mind's ability to know. We are incapable of knowing anything beyond the wonders of our daily lives. There is enough mystery and beauty—and suffering—in the lives we live. To be as fully alive as possible—to be compassionate with ourselves and with others—is enough religion for a lifetime. Down on the farm we lived close to the earth.

The Atlantic voyage of Bridget and John from Ireland recedes with the generations. The ways of the Irish—the Hail Marys, the masses at St. Andrews, the clay pipes, the work clothes—are only ghostly reminders. Kate's black rosary beads, escaping the burial, lie scattered on the attic floor. Spirits find haven in the curious minds and souls of the descendents.

*E*ACH SUMMER we took a vacation to northern Wisconsin. The trip was planned to coincide with our father's worst attacks of hay fever and asthma. He had been afflicted ever since stacking moldy hay in the barn as a young man, compounded by an allergy to ragweed. We would get in the car and head for Rice Lake. Late one summer afternoon, while driving, mother raced the Hiawatha for several miles on the highway that paralleled the track. We would, with fond humor, remind her of that day for the rest of her life.

Summer would end with the Walworth County Fair, always held the weekend of Labor Day. When young, before they knew each other, our mother and father would attend the fair, driving to the fairgrounds in Elkhorn in horse and buggy. In our youth, the fair was a vacation from farm work. It was the time we would show our calves, hogs, sheep, and chickens in 4-H competition. Among the photographs, I find a fading newspaper clipping showing me—in a close-up pose—with a chicken in my arms. Under the photo, the caption reads:

> A consistent winner in poultry competition at the Walworth County fair is Earl Quinney, Sugar Creek 4-H member, shown above with this blue ribbon barred rock cockerel. He won four blues in Friday judging, and stands a chance to receive the championship award in 4-H poultry in bankers' night ceremonies—an honor he has won for the past two years.

On Monday night, the last night of the fair, we would load our livestock into the truck, knowing that summer had ended. And we knew that the seasons to follow would hold other delights. Dunham School closed its doors at the end of the 1947 school year. We few remaining students were transferred to the Island School two miles west of the farm. The move to the new school and my graduation in the spring of 1948 marked the end of the old life on the farm.

The great transition and adjustment to high school in town took me farther and farther away from the farm. I am in the driver's seat of the pickup truck, about to leave the farm for the beginning of my second year at Delavan High School. The year is 1950, and my mother records the departure with box camera in hand. I have been granted a special permit for students needing to drive to school.

Driving to high school, first day of the school year, 1950

Two worlds divided, the kids from town and the kids from the country. We of the country were readily labeled as being "farmers." For the four years in Delavan High School, I struggled to compensate for being from the country and to be accepted by the kids in town. After the first year, I developed severe stomach pains, and sought relief by convincing my doctor that I needed to have my appendix removed. The operation—with a perfectly good appendix removed—prepared me for the next three years of high school. I was elected to office in the student body, learned to play trombone in the band, played golf, wrote and photographed for the student newspaper, and appeared in a school play. I was even invited to the house of one of the town students to watch General Douglas MacArthur on television deliver his old-soldiers-never-die speech before Congress. I was making it in town.

I graduated from high school in 1952, went to college and to graduate school, and spent the subsequent years in a series of academic jobs that would take me to places far away from the farm.

WITH THE CAR HEADED OUT OF THE DRIVEWAY, but stuck in drifts of newly fallen snow, I shouted to my father that I was leaving this God-forsaken place and that I was never coming back. He hooked the log chain to the car and with the Oliver tractor pulled the car to the road. Returning to college, I knew I was on my way away from the farm. And yet, no matter how far I traveled, or how long I stayed away, I never left the farm and the farm never left me. Late in life—now—I return weekly to the farm and to the place that future generations will continue to call the Old Place.

Even away at college, I longed to be home at night in the farmhouse. I missed the quietness at bedtime, and the soft voices bidding me good night. I worried that I would never to able to leave home. Still, I did not want to be a farmer. I wanted to move to town and to travel throughout the world. Soon I was married, and with the birth of two daughters, Laura and Anne, I had a family. I was a professor, teaching in a series of universities, and living finally in New York City. My father had often sung the song while we were working in the fields—"How 'Ya Gonna Keep 'Em Down on the Farm After They've Seen Paree?"

All the while I would return to the farm to visit my mother and father and to walk the familiar and much-loved grounds of the farm. Gradually, as my father and mother got older, they reduced the amount of work on the farm. My father died in the fall of 1969, two weeks after visiting us in New York City and telling us that he did not have long to live. I told him no, that he would live for a long time. My mother continued to live alone on the farm for the next thirty years. I was with her the morning she died, helping her prepare for an appointment with her doctor. She died at home and escaped having to leave the farm to live someplace else.

Now, I live sixty miles north of the farm. Solveig and I go down to the farm weekly. We tend the house, plant the garden, see that the fields are prepared and harvested, and have hopes that the farm can be preserved. Ralph comes to make repairs on the barn and chicken house, and keeps the records. We all walk to the marsh and to the fields that have been planted with hardwood seedlings and with prairie grasses and forbs. Gradually the farmland is being converted to sustainable agriculture. The whole farm is becoming an integral part of the natural world. How many times have I told friends that I have spent a lifetime trying to get away from the farm? Now there is no need: I live daily knowing that the farm and I are one.

THIS IS THE STORY I continue to tell. I have the apparent need to keep telling it, trying to remember, trying not to forget how I got from there to here. As memory of the past fades, I have the accumulated stories to help me remember. It is not that I think that the past is better than the present, or that I want to be back there again. Rather, it is by recognizing the past that I am better able to live in the present.

What I have remembered—and what I have told—is not a lament. I do miss and have great sorrow for loved ones now gone. But I also celebrate their lives and am pleased for their lives. We all have our entrances and our exits. And in our time we play our many parts and live our varied lives. With good fortune, we will be remembered, just as we remember those who came before us.

Still Life

In a sense, one never leaves home. Home is where you start from, as T. S. Eliot noted in his poem, and home stays with you for the rest of your life. I spent my teen and early adult years trying to extricate myself from that home on the farm in Wisconsin. I am surprised to find that over a half-century later I have returned to the farm, and that I am spending much of my time and energy trying to preserve the 160 acres of farmland, woods, marsh, and the buildings that remain in various stages of decay and repair. Even among the ruins—especially among the ruins—I find a depth of meaning. As I get older, the world becomes stranger, and more wondrous for all of that.

Weekly, at least, I mount the camera to the tripod and go to the old places on the farm. My self-imposed project is to photograph the artifacts, to make a record of the things that remain of the life that once was here. Each photograph is in the artistic tradition of the still life, where the material things of everyday life are portrayed in repose, indicating the transience of this earthly existence. These material things, devoid of their former purpose and function, receive my attention and care. These old and inanimate things now have an afterlife as they rest among the ruins.

Years of experience, travel, thought and spiritual life have brought me to this present place. I am fortunate to be in the place that has been a constant source of my life, no matter how far I have wandered away. This is the place that is grounded in the past of my ancestors, a place that carries me into the present. A wider world is known only as it begins here.

I CONTINUE TO BE HAUNTED by the sense of place. And not only by the sense of place, but also by this place to which I am native. My personal history, the history of my family, and the history of the immigrant culture of which I am part, all give emotional and spiritual weight to what I know and experience as place. For place is charged with the opposing forces of movement and settlement. When one moves, one wants to get settled; when settled, we anticipate a move. Restless, we keep moving no matter how settled we become.

I have spent my life living with the great dynamic of moving and staying. As I have moved about, hundreds of miles from the place of my birth, I have carried with me a sense of home that can be experienced anywhere. Yet there is always the tension between the ideal of living in the house I was born in and the desire for movement in my life that comes with transport to another place. Wherever I have lived, I have tried to know—I have had the need to know—the new location as a place. I am informed by Wallace Stegner's notion of place, defined in his book *Where the Bluebird Sings to the Lemonade Springs:* "A place is not a place until people have been born in it, have grown up in it, lived in it, known it, died in it—have experienced and shaped it, as individuals, families, neighborhoods, and communities, over more than one generation."

My places are the places I have lived in over the course of a lifetime, as well as the place I left to begin my life as an adult. My home place, finally at this stage of my life, is the place I have been searching for all my life. It is the Old Place at the farm, and the territory that radiates from it—Chicago to the south, Madison and the Wisconsin River to the north, Lake Michigan to the east, and an unlimited stretch of land to the west. This is the home country.

I have reverence for the past, certainly, but I am not nostalgic for what no longer exists. The present is now my home place. I know that I am fortunate to be here.

Since my mother died, leaving the farm to my brother and me, we have been working on ways to preserve the farm. Several acres of hilly farmland—"the alps" north of the Old Place—have been placed in the Conservation Reserve Program. Clusters of hardwood trees—oaks and hickory—have been planted on the hills. Prairie grasses have been planted on the hills and valleys—grasses commonly known as Big Bluestem, Canada Wild Rye, Switch Grass, Little Bluestem, and Indian Grass. Twenty-five types of Wisconsin native forbs were planted with the grasses, including Purple Prairie Clover, Butterfly Weed, Compass Plant, Purple Coneflower, Goldenrod, White Wild Indigo,

The farm from the corner of Quinney Road

Prairie Dock, Sky Blue Aster, Foxglove, Western Sunflower, and Wild Garlic. Future generations will walk through fields of prairie grass and rest in the shade of the hardwood trees.

We are converting the acres of farmland—about 100 acres—to sustainable agriculture. The aim is to turn the whole farm—agricultural and otherwise—into a natural habitat. This means moving from the techniques of industrial-type farming which have contaminated the land with pesticides and herbicides, to natural and sustainable methods. The ponds and marshes, which have always been brooding areas for wildlife, will be improved for wildlife habitation. In addition, biologists and ecologists will be using the farm as a research and teaching location—covering the areas of aquatic and field biology, entomology, ornithology, and animal behavior. The objective of all these activities is to preserve the farm, to keep it as an open space, to improve the natural habitat, and to honor our ancestors.

With the income received annually from the crops, we are able to pay the taxes and make the necessary repairs. The farmhouse is being maintained. The fate of the other buildings, including the large barn, is uncertain. Some of the buildings, the chicken house and the sheep shed, are already beyond repair as they begin to turn into ruins. We will let them stand, or fall as they may—bearing witness to the life that once was here. My life—and perhaps that of future generations—could not exist without the farm.

I AM INSPIRED by the book *The Dickinsons of Amherst.* The book contains contemplative essays on Emily Dickinson's family as they lived in their houses in Amherst, Massachusetts. Throughout the book are the beautiful photographs by Jerome Liebling of the houses and the artifacts that remain untouched since the rooms were filled with the lives of the Dickinson family. The photographs are of the aesthetic of the spirit photographs of a century and a half ago.

As Liebling photographed the remains, he was preoccupied

with what can be called the afterlife of things. The dresses of Emily Dickinson are still hanging in the upstairs closet. They assume a strange expressiveness that goes far beyond the material world. It is as if the inanimate objects still possess some of the life of the ones who once used them. As if some small portion of Emily's life is contained in the abandoned dresses, and is contained in the photographs that we observers view many years later. Of course, it is we who remain who give meaning to the objects and the images. But we are ready to entertain the possibility that something—call it spirit—remains in the material world of things.

The silo filler stored in the barn

With camera and tripod, I go into the barn and climb to the dark haymow. Stretched out on a high beam, a raccoon watches as I study the light and make my exposures on film. Piles of hay are stacked in corners, remaining from the time the milking of the

Haymow

Dad's workbench in the machine shed

Egg crate, pump, and pail in the chicken house

cows ceased on the farm. Below are the stanchions where cows once stood patiently. At the far end of the barn is the stall where the great Holstein bull watched our every move.

In the large metal machine shed, I photograph the artifacts from the work and play of another time. I take great care in photographing the workbench where my father last stood on the cold November day he died nearly forty years ago. A light gently falls over the workbench.

I go to what once was the chicken house, tended for years by my mother, and I photograph the tools and various other objects abandoned after they were no longer of any use. In the building that once housed a variety of animals, hang the bridle and feedbag once worn by the horses on the farm.

In the basement of the farmhouse, I photograph the artifacts hanging on the walls. Upstairs, I frame in the viewfinder of my camera the rooms and furnishings that served another time. With tripod and camera over my shoulder, I climb to the attic of the farmhouse to photograph while I still have the light of day. Perhaps this is as much of the afterlife that I will ever know.

As I look at the artifacts, walking carefully among rusting tools and decaying matters, stepping between the droppings of raccoons and woodchucks, sometimes wearing a paper mask to protect me from the dust and mold—stopping to photograph when something meets the eye of this beholder—I wonder if all this is the ending of an era that has stretched for nearly a hundred and fifty years on this place that I continue to call home. Am I the last of this line to bear witness to those emigrants who left the old world in escape from famine and economic depression searching for something else? Exploring a dark corner in one of the old buildings, I see myself as one of

Horse feedbag in the sheep shed

Sled and milk cans in the basement of the farmhouse

The attic with an ancestor's portrait

Dad's winter coat in the attic

the ancient ones, a mariner of sorts, left over from a life that once was here. I am haunted by the mysteries of time and place.

Fortunate I am to have my camera to see into the afterlife of things. Often I am beyond the expression of words. I think about the writer James Agee as he once sat in a shack trying to write about the things his friend Walker Evans was photographing around him. With a spontaneous flow of words, a stream of consciousness as much as thought, Agee wrote the following in *Let Us Now Praise Famous Men:* "If I could do it, I'd do no writing at all here. It would be photographs; the rest would be fragments of cloth, bits of cotton, lumps of earth, records of speech, pieces of wool and iron, phials of odors, plates of food, and excrement."

The worn winter coat that once my father wore when hauling loads of milk on winter days hangs in the dark corner of the attic in the farmhouse. Canning jars, once containing the preserves prepared for the family by my mother sixty years ago, line the shelves in the fruit cellar. The artifacts from the lives that once were lived here—in this place I continue to call home.

Canning jars in the fruit cellar

THE PHOEBES have been tending their nest since the early days of spring. A nest of fibers and mud clings to the corner of the porch under the eave of the farmhouse. Four feathered babies now perch on the edge of the nest, about to take flight.

Phoebes are at the center of Robert Frost's poem "The Need of Being Versed in Country Things." In the poem, a farm has been abandoned, left in ruins from fire and decay. A chimney is all that remains from the house; the barn stands forsaken, the sounds of horse hooves on the floor long gone. We humans easily lament the passing of the years and the falling to ruin of what once housed precious life. But among the phoebes there is little lament. Frost's poem ends:

> For them there was really nothing sad.
> But though they rejoiced in the nest they kept
> One had to be versed in country things
> Not to believe the phoebes wept.

Making my way among the ruins, I take little comfort in being versed in country things.

The living room in the farmhouse

My mother's Bible has come to rest on the corner of the table in the living room of the farmhouse. Her mother and father inscribed it to her in 1917 when she was eleven. A bookmark had been placed at the beginning of Ecclesiastes. "To everything there is a season, and a time to every purpose under the heaven: a time to be born, and a time to die; a time to plant, and a time to pluck up that which is planted." The Bible is filled with newspaper clippings, church bulletins, obituaries, and pamphlets accumulated over the years. My mother saved these words near the end of her life: "We are today's seniors. A hardy bunch when you think of how our world has changed and the adjustments we had to make!"

I never asked my mother for her thoughts and beliefs about death. She once told me that she had never thought that she would live to be in her nineties. My memory is of a person who chose to live fully rather than spend time worrying about death. I am trying to do the same. Without a myth for some consolation about death, living the mystery of life continues to be my spiritual path. Death is the price we pay for living in this world. My explorations are of the wonders in the present time.

*T*HE SUMMER, as with all summers, ends with the Walworth County Fair. The summer vegetables have been judged and assigned ribbons. Farm animals have been shown in the coliseum, and 4-H'ers are gathering around the barns late into the night. The giant Ferris wheel adorned with colored lights is turning against the sky. We make certain to walk through the poultry barn on our way out of the fairgrounds. School will begin tomorrow morning, the day after the fair. Much of time present, even with its spontaneous and extraordinary moments, follows a storyline.

We pick the remainder of the garden's summer crop. I complete the last photographs of the ruins and artifacts of the farm, carefully opening the granary doors and photographing the wagon deep in dust. Jars of tomato sauce and salsa are stacked into the cupboard for use this winter. I go down to the Old Place and pick the wild grapes on the vines that drape over shrubs and trees. Back in the farmhouse, we boil the grapes, add sugar and pectin, and pour the rich blue liquid into jars that will for a time preserve the summer's sun.

Among the ruins
As winter comes—
Still life
On the farm.

Chronology

1821 Birth of John Quinney, County Kilkenny, Ireland
1827 James Wishart and Joyce Taylor emigrate from England
1831 Birth of Bridget O'Keefe, County Kilkenny, Ireland
1839 Birth of James Holloway, North Devon, England
1845 Birth of Mary Bray, Devonshire, England
1846 Bridget O'Keefe emigrates to New York
1849 John Quinney emigrates to New York
1850 Marriage of John Quinney and Bridget O'Keefe in Yonkers
1851 George Taylor and Ann Crooks emigrate from England
1851 Birth of Ellen (Nellie) Wishart
1853 Birth of Charles Taylor
1855 Birth of Katherine Quinney
1857 Birth of Thomas Quinney
1859 John and Bridget Quinney move to Wisconsin
1860 Birth of John H. Quinney
1864 Birth of William Quinney
1865 Birth of Mary Quinney; James Holloway emigrates on the S.S. Damascus
1867 Walter Bray and Rachael Baker Bray emigrate from England
1868 John and Bridget Quinney purchase the Old Place
1870 Birth of Hattie Reynolds, Rock County, Wisconsin
1871 Marriage of James Holloway and Mary Bray
1872 Birth of William V. B. Holloway, Walworth County, Wisconsin
1880 Death of John Quinney; Thomas Quinney moves to South Dakota
1883 Birth of Lorena Taylor, Walworth County, Wisconsin
1887 William Quinney moves to South Dakota

1895 Birth of Marjorie Quinney
1900 Birth of Floyd Quinney
1903 Marriage of W. V. B. Holloway and Lorena Taylor
1904 Birth of Nellie Quinney
1905 Death of Hattie Quinney
1906 Birth of Alice Marie Holloway; death of Nellie Quinney
1911 Death of James Holloway
1919 Death of Nellie Taylor
1920 Death of Bridget Quinney
1921 Death of Lorena Taylor Holloway
1922 Death of Mary Bray Holloway
1924 Floyd Quinney travels to California; death of Thomas Quinney
1924 Marriage of W. V. B. Holloway and Mabel Stiles
1930 Marriage of Floyd Quinney and Alice Holloway
1931 Death of Charles Taylor
1934 Birth of Earl Richard Quinney
1935 Death of Marjorie Quinney
1936 Birth of Ralph Douglas Quinney; death of William Quinney
1939 Death of John Quinney
1941 Death of Mary Quinney Reynolds
1942 Death of Katherine Quinney
1948 Earl Richard Quinney graduates from grade school
1950 Ralph Quinney graduates from grade school
1959 Death of W. V. B. Holloway
1969 Death of Floyd Quinney
1999 Death of Alice Quinney
2004 Transition to sustainable agriculture

Ancestor Chart

- *Earl Richard Quinney (1934–) and Ralph Quinney (1936–)*
  - *Floyd Quinney (1900–1969)*
    - *John Quinney (1860–1939)*
      - *John Quinney (1821–1880)*
      - *Bridget O'Keefe (1831–1920)*
    - *Hattie Reynolds (1870–1905)*
      - *Nathan Church Reynolds (1828–1895)*
      - *Mary Potter (1832–1910)*
        - *Jonathan Potter (1799–1870)*
        - *Mary Swain (1800–1832)*
  - *Alice Marie Holloway (1906–1999)*
    - *W.V.B. Holloway (1872–1959)*
      - *James Holloway (1839–1911)*
        - *William Holloway (unknown)*
        - *Ann Verney (unknown)*
      - *Mary Bray (1845–1922)*
        - *Walter Bray (1813–1887)*
        - *Rachel Baker (1817–1895)*
    - *Lorena Taylor (1883–1921)*
      - *Charles Taylor (1853–1931)*
        - *George Taylor (1826–1896)*
        - *Ann Crooks (1833–1898)*
      - *Ellen (Nellie) Wishart (1851–1919)*
        - *James Wishart (unknown)*
        - *Joyce Taylor (unknown)*

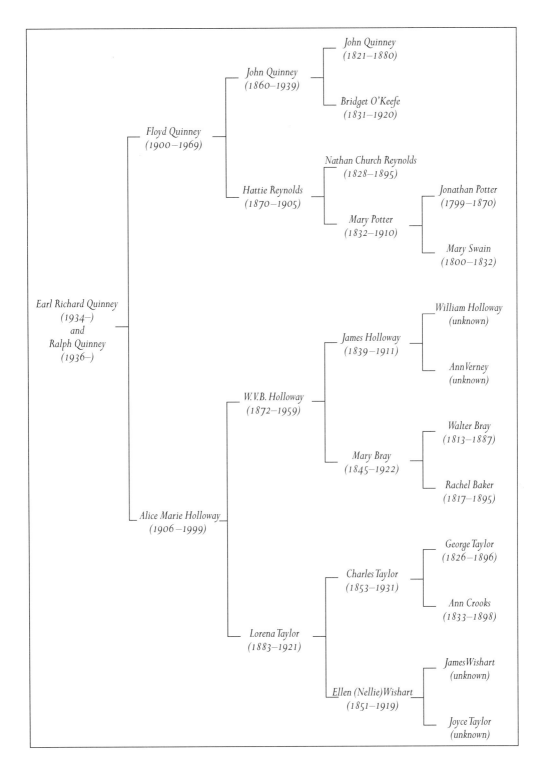

Photographs

Page No.

Bibliography

The following books provided an intellectual and aesthetic context for the writing of this book.

Agee, James and Walker Evans. *Let Us Now Praise Famous Men.* Boston: Houghton Mifflin, 1941.
Barthes, Roland. *Camera Lucida: Reflections on Photography.* Trans. Richard Howard. New York: Hill and Wang, 1981.
Berger, John and Jean Mohr. *A Fortunate Man.* New York: Pantheon Books, 1967.
Berry, Wendell. *A Timbered Choir: The Sabbath Poems 1979–1997.* Washington: Counterpoint, 1998.
Chaucer, Geoffrey. *The Canterbury Tales.* Trans. Nevill Coghill. Baltimore: Penguin Books, 1962.
Coleridge, Samuel Taylor. *The Rime of the Ancient Mariner.* Ed. Paul H. Fry. Boston: Bedford/St.Martin's, 1999.
Delano, Jack. *Photographic Memories.* Washington, DC: Smithsonian Institution Press, 1997.
Donnelly, James S., Jr. *The Great Irish Potato Famine.* Gloucestershire, England: Sutton Publishing, 2001.
Eliot, T. S. *The Complete Poems and Plays of T. S. Eliot.* London: Faber and Faber, 1969.
Frost, Robert. *Collected Poems, Prose, and Plays.* New York: Library of America, 1995.
Garland, Hamlin. *Main-Travelled Roads.* New York: Macmillan, 1891.
Garland, Hamlin. *A Son of the Middle Border.* Lincoln: University of Nebraska Press, 1979. [1917]
Heaney, Seamus. *Finders Keepers: Selected Prose, 1971–2001.* New York: Farrar, Straus and Giroux, 2002.
Hirsch, Marianne. *Family Frames: Photography, Narrative, and Postmemory.* Cambridge: Harvard University Press, 1997.
Jackson, J. B. *The Necessity of Ruins.* Amherst: University of Massachusetts Press, 1980.
Kaplan, Laura Duhan. *Family Pictures: A Philosopher Explores the Familiar.* Chicago: Open Court, 1998.
LaGrange Pioneers. Walworth County: LaGrange Ladies' Aid Society, 1935.
Leopold, Aldo. *A Sand County Almanac.* New York: Oxford University Press, 1949.

Lesy, Michael. *Wisconsin Death Trip.* New York: Pantheon Books, 1973.
Liebling, Jerome, Christopher Benfry, Polly Longsworth and Barton St. Armand, *The Dickinsons of Amherst.* Hanover: University Press of New England, 2001.
Logan, Ben. *The Land Remembers.* New York: Viking Press, 1975.
Logsdon, Gene. *The Contrary Farmer.* White River Junction, VT: Chelsea Green Publishing Co., 1994.
Masters, Edgar Lee. *Spoon River Anthology.* Ed. John E. Hallwas. Urbana: University of Illinois Press, 1992. [1915]
Naipaul, V. S. *Literary Occasions: Essays.* Intro. and ed. Pankaj Mishra. New York: Alfred A. Knopf, 2003.
Quinney, Richard. *Borderland: A Midwest Journal.* Madison: University of Wisconsin Press, 2001.
Quinney, Richard. *Journey to a Far Place.* Philadelphia: Temple University Press, 1991.
Quinney, Richard. *Where Yet the Sweet Birds Sing.* Madison, WI: Borderland Books, 2006.
Shunryu Suzuki. *Zen Mind, Beginner's Mind.* New York: Weatherhill, 1970.
Sontag, Susan. *On Photography.* New York: Farrar, Straus and Giroux, 1977.
Stegner, Wallace. *Where the Bluebird Sings to the Lemonade Springs.* New York: Random House, 1992.
Sudek, Josef. *Josef Sudek, Poet of Prague: A Photographer's Life.* Biographical Profile by Anna Farova. New York: Aperture, 1990.
Travis, David. *Edward Weston: The Last Years in Carmel.* Chicago: Art Institute of Chicago, 2001.
Vendler, Helen. *The Art of Shakespeare's Sonnets.* Cambridge: Harvard University Press, 1997.
Wang, Wei. *Laughing Lost in the Mountains: Poems of Wang Wei.* Trans. Tony Barnstone, Willis Barnstone, and Xu Haixin. Hanover: University Press of New England, 1991.
Wescott, Glenway. *Good-Bye Wisconsin.* New York: Harper, 1928.
Wolfe, Linnie Marsh. *Son of the Wilderness: The Life of John Muir.* New York: Alfred A. Knopf, 1945.
Wordsworth, William. *The Poems of William Wordsworth.* Ed. Jonathan Wordsworth. Cambridge, England: University Printing House, 1973.

About the Author

RICHARD QUINNEY is the author of several books that combine autobiographical writing and photography, including *Journey to a Far Place, For the Time Being, Borderland, Once Again the Wonder,* and *Where Yet the Sweet Birds Sing.* His other books are in the academic field of sociology. He and his wife live in Madison, Wisconsin, and on the family farm in Walworth County.

This book is set in Adobe Garamond, a digital interpretation by Robert Slimbach of the sixteenth-century roman types of Claude Garamond and the italic types of Robert Granjon, and Perpetua, designed by Eric Gil. It was designed by Ken Crocker, printed at The Stinehour Press, and bound by Acme Bookbinding. The paper is 80 lb. Cougar Opaque Natural Smooth.